REHABILITATION OF CHILD LABOUR

REHABILITATION OF CHILD LABOUR

Problems and Prospects

(With Special Reference to Kashmir)

Bilal Bhat

SHIPRA

ISBN: 978-81-7541-581-2

First Published in India in 2011

Rehabilitation of Child Labour: Problems and Prospects

Published by:
SHIPRA PUBLICATIONS
H.O.: LG 18-19, Pankaj Central Market, Patparganj,
I.P. Ext., Delhi-110092, Tel: 91-11-2223 5152, 2223 6152
Br.Off.: 4617/18, Ansari Road, Darya Ganj,
New Delhi-110002, Tel: 6594 6453, 9810522367
E-mail: info@shiprapublications.com
www.shiprapublications.com

PREFACE

Children have been typified as fountainheads of knowledge, apparition and activities. But how effective can the participation of children be under conditions where even most of the adults cannot aver rights to whittle in? There apparently is an apprehension, if not a conflict, between stressing the agency of the individual (child) and stressing the importance for structural changes which will enable all (children) to move on to a level field.

There is a growing theoretical and empirical literature concerning the causes and consequences of child labour. The objective of this study is to evaluate the policy initiatives targeted on child labour in light of the newly emerging theoretical argumentation and empirical evidence. We focus in particular on programs to address child-labor practices, and we attempt to evaluate these programs, given the empirical evidence concerning the primary determinants of when and why children work. Throughout, we find it instructive to evaluate the policies that have been adopted with the intent of reducing overall child labor in terms of the impact they are likely to have on the welfare of the children.

Most people want to study child labour because they want to improve children's conditions. They do this by asking a lot of questions about why children work, about school and education and how it is related to work, about whether children have to work, about who sends them to work, about the nature and conditions of their work, about who benefits from their work, about their health status, and even about whether work for children might be a good thing. We discuss some of these questions in this book. Some are self-evident, but others that might appear clear-cut at first glance turn out to be rather complex.

The spectre of small children toiling long hours under dehumanizing conditions has precipitated an intense debate concerning child labour over the past decade and a half. As during the midst of the 19th century industrial revolution, policy makers and the public have attempted to come to grips with the causes and consequences of child labour. Coordinating a policy response has revealed the complexity and moral ambiguity of the phenomenon of working children.

Although child labour has been the norm throughout history, the fact of children working and the difficult conditions under which children work occasionally became more evident. In the midst of the 19th century, child labour became more visible because children were drawn into an industrial setting. Currently, child labour has become more visible because of the increase in the number of children producing goods for export.

Our purpose here is not only to provide a definitive diagnosis of the causes and consequences of child labour, but also to review the existing theoretical, empirical and historical literature as to why and when children work. As will become clear, technology and other demand side factors interact subtly with household dynamics, culture, and market and political failures to determine the labour force participation rate and educational attainment of children.

In chapter II and III, we review the theoretical literature and some incidental empirical evidence concerning household decision-making and its implications for work and school choices for children. Unitary models are analyzed first, followed by models with multiple agencies. We consider household decision making, itself, along with market characteristics that constrain the choices that families make concerning their children in chapter IV. In particular, considerable recent theoretical and empirical attention has focussed on the role that market failures play in child labour. Failures that emerge in financial, spot labour, and human capital markets can all give rise to more child labour than is economically efficient or in the interest of the families. We will also find that political failure can play a significant role in determining the allocation of children's time. We then turn, in chapter VI, to a discussion of the empirical evidence on these and other related issues based on field study in different parts of Kashmir.

The methodological aspect of the study is broached in chapter V. Here we consider the role the tools and techniques used in the study for researching the problem play in discussing and debating the child labour. This chapter within its framework also includes various approaches towards the study of child labour i.e. social and humanitarian and the methodology adopted in conducting the research. The final chapter of the study summarises the findings and then concludes the study. It also includes recommendations and suggestions for the solution of the problem.

Amid a plethora of literature on working children, the present work on the same subject is distinguished by its extensiveness and holistic treatment. Not only that a considerable number of child labourers were interviewed but their employers and parents were also interviewed to make the study multidimensional and objective in character. In-depth interviews with government officials and social workers were also taken. The case studies at the end of the findings chapter help to provide a holistic picture of the problem. We are sure this work will provide a very valuable addition to the vast literature on working children, besides being useful to those directly working with such problems.

Rehabilitation of child labourers' problems and prospects has been produced to help policy-makers to ensure that handicrafts, agriculture, domestic work, etc. are priority sectors for the elimination of child labour. The manual included in this sheathe provide policy-makers and stakeholder organizations – employers' organizations, trade unions, occupational safety and health agencies/institutions, agricultural agencies and others with information and ideas needed to plan, formulate and implement policies and programmes to tackle hazardous child labour. It contains a comprehensive resource and reference material intended to address the needs of a variety of key audiences, especially partner organizations.

As much of the work these children do is considered as "helping out", it is seldom recognized in official statistics. Thus, the real extent of the problem may be invisible to policy-makers. It is often the head of the household who is registered as working in agriculture, handicrafts, etc. Child labour in handicrafts, tourism, agriculture, etc. may also go unnoticed when underage workers are supplied through labour contractors and sub-contractors. The "family farm" element in agriculture and handicrafts that is universal and bound-up with culture and tradition can make it both difficult to acknowledge that children can be exploited in such a setting as well as a no-go area for child labour action. Handicrafts, domestic work and agriculture, etc. are also historically and traditionally an under-regulated sectors in many countries. This means that child labour laws – if only they exist – are often less stringent than for other types of work. The prevalence of child labour in these sectors also undermines decent work, sustainable agriculture, rural development and food security as it perpetuates a cycle of poverty where household income for both farmers and waged workers is insufficient to meet their economic needs. As with other forms of child labour, handicrafts, domestic work, agricultural work, etc. can also impede children's access to education and/or skills training and limit their possibilities of economic and social mobility and advancement in later life.

It is because of these factors – large numbers, the hazardous nature of the work, early age of entry into labour, invisibility, lack of regulation, poverty and denial of education – that handicrafts and agriculture, must be priority areas for the elimination of child labour. However, social mobilization leading to action to eliminate child labour is a relatively underdeveloped area of child labour. So it is with a view to encouraging the expansion of work to eliminate hazardous child labour that this publication has been produced. It provides guidance to a wide audience from policy-makers to practitioners. We wish every success in the efforts to eliminate child labour.

I would like to express my very warm gratitude to my teachers T. A. Rather and B. A. Dabla, who each read a draft of the first edition and made extensive comments. Their advice and criticism was both constructive and insightful, and undoubtedly improved the book, deepening and sharpening discussion at a number of points. My publisher, D. Kumar, has been a constant source of enthusiasm, encouragement and support. My friends and colleagues were closely involved at every stage in the production of the book. I would be remiss if I did not make special mention of the contribution faculty CCAS and Sociology and Social Work made for the present study. My sincere thanks to child labourers in the handicraft centres, workshops, agriculture, hotels and restaurants, etc. their parents and employers who have extended their cooperation in furnishing the information needed for the present study. This venture would not have been possible but for love, sacrifice, patience and encouragement of my parents. I have no words to express my thanks to them. I also place on record my sincere and grateful thanks to all those authors and writers from whose writings I have been benefited. In the end, of course, there is no one but me to blame for the mistakes and I am left with the niggling feeling that somehow I haven't said quite what I meant.

Bhat Bilal Ahmad

CONTENTS

LIST OF ABBREVIATIONS

BPL	:	Below Poverty Line
CCCL	:	Centre of Concern for Child Labour
CRC	:	Convention on the Rights of the Child
CSR	:	Centre for Social Research
FRDPSP	:	Fundamental Rights, Directive Principles of State Policy
GDP	:	Grass Domestic Product
GMACL	:	Global March Against Child Labour
GO	:	Government Organization
GO	:	Government Official
HRD	:	Human Resource Development
HTW	:	Half Time Working
ICSSR	:	Indian Council of Social Science Research
ILO	:	International Labour Organization
IPEC	:	International Programme on the Elimination of Child Labour
IYC	:	International Year of the Child
J&K	:	Jammu and Kashmir
MAC	:	Minimum Age Convention
MOU	:	Memorandum of Understanding
NAECL	:	National Authority for the Elimination of Child Labour
NAP	:	National Action Plan
NCLP	:	National Child Labour Projects
NGO	:	Non Governmental Organization
NIEPA	:	National Institute for Educational Planning and Administration
NSSO	:	National Sample Survey Organization
ORG	:	Operation Research Group
PPP	:	Purchasing Power Parity
SC	:	Schedule Caste
SNA	:	System of National Accounts
ST	:	Schedule Tribe
SW	:	Social Worker
UNESCO	:	United Nations Educational, Scientific and Cultural Organization
UNICEF	:	United Nations Children's Fund
UNO	:	United Nations Organization
US	:	United States
WFCL	:	Worst Forms of Child Labour

1

INTRODUCTION

The conduit and secretarial technicalities of development espoused by different countries may be varied but an effectual utilization of human resource is a normative standard as growth and development is the key concern of all nations. The child cannot develop into a full-blown human being, unless productive and amiable environment is assured for his/her development. He/she is to be provided planned care and adequate socialization opportunities in order to enable him/her to attain human status. He/she is susceptible to environmental bullying, so his/her survival and health requirements must be met first. His/her cognitive and emotional development has to be braced with spur surroundings, love, affection, human warmth and security.[1]

In developing countries, children have always been the responsibility of the primary institution of society, viz. family. The traditional care lavished on children, has suffered erosion because of new constraints and consequently abuse and exploitation of child has become common place. The plight of the child has been further aggravated by the endemic and entrenched poverty. Inspite of the constitutional measures and number of welfare development schemes for them, a sizeable proportion of child population is still working as wage labourers/apprentices, paid/unpaid both in urban and rural areas in very deplorable and inhuman conditions.

The prevalence of child labour is not a recent phenomenon. Even in the ancient times children were put to arduous labour in houses and in fields at an early age. Performances of tasks like tending of cattle, collection of grass and fuel etc. by children relieve the adult members of the family for more productive work. There was no social labour against children working along with their parents. It was this factor of child labour which strongly established family and kinship ties in occupations. In the urban areas, because of their poverty many parents not only cannot make any investment in their children's development but they are also reluctant to support them. They want their children to find work for themselves as early as possible. The employers prefer children as they are more agile, amenable to discipline and control and are cheaper and more adoptive.

The problematic aspect of child labour became more pronounced with the advent of industrial era. Being in the labour, such children are denied educational opportunities; their physical, mental and intellectual development is hampered. The working children generally remain unskilled, underpaid, under-privileged throughout life, their physical and social mobility get restricted and vicious and cumulative cycle of poverty, ill-health, under employment and unemployment also get strengthened.[2]

Child labour problem with multidimensional implications is one among the many crucial problems faced by the developing nations and India is no exception to this. In the early phase of industrialization child labour suffered most brutal and unprecedented exploitation in the western world though its intensity has considerably been lessened in the advanced industrial nations now. In India, the problem by and large has lost its poignancy in the organized and public sector of employment but it has assumed alarming proportion in the unorganized and unregulated sectors. Normatively child labour has serious consequences and implications for children, parents and families and as such it has been recognized as a social evil.[3]

Concept of Child Labour

Defining child labour is not as simple and straightforward as it may appear because it encompasses three difficult-to-define concepts "child", "work", and "labour". Childhood can be defined in terms of age. In some societies, age may not be a sufficient basis for defining "childhood". The fulfilment of certain social rites and traditional obligations may well be important requirements in defining "adult" and "child" status. In still others, the integration of children into socio-economic life may begin so early that it may be virtually impossible to identify clearly the different life phases. Besides, in the absence of an effective age record system, even applying an agreed legal definition becomes highly problematic. However, in the context of child labour, a working definition of a "child" may be a person below the general limit of fifteen years or in special circumstances fourteen years, set by the Minimum Age Convention, 1973 (No. 138).

The term child labour is often defined as work that deprives children of their childhood, their potential and their dignity, and that is harmful to physical and mental development. It refers to work that:

- Is mentally, physically, socially or morally dangerous and harmful to children: and
- Interferes with their schooling.
  - by depriving them of the opportunity to attend school;
  - by obliging them to leave school prematurely; or
  - by requiring them to attempt to combine school attendance with excessively long and heavy work.

In its most extreme forms, child labour involves children being enslaved, separated from their families, exposed to serious hazards and illness and/or left to fend for themselves on the streets of large cities-often at a very early age. Whether or not particular forms of 'work' can be called 'child labour' depends on the child's age, the type and hours of work performed, the conditions under which it is performed and the objectives pursued by individual countries.[4]

According to Francis Blanchard (former director of ILO) "Child Labour includes children prematurely leading adult lives, working long hours for low wages under conditions damaging to their health and to their physical and mental development, Sometimes separated from their families, frequently deprived of education and training apprentices that could provide them a better future".[5]

According to Homer Folks, the chairman of the US National Child Labour Committee, the term 'child labour' is generally used to refer, "any work by children that interfere with their full physical and mental development, the opportunities for a desirable minimum of education and of their needed recreation".[6]

UNICEF has given a comprehensive formulation in its attempt at defining child labour:

1. Starting full-time work at too early an age.
2. Working too long within or outside the family and unable to attend school.
3. Work resulting in excessive physical, social and psychological strains upon the child as in the case of sexual exploitation and dangerous work as military service and mining.
4. Work on the street is unhealthy and dangerous,
5. Inadequate remuneration for working outside the family, as in the case of the child workers in carpet weaving.
6. Too much responsibility at too early an age as in the domestic situation.
7. Work does not facilitate the psychological and social development of the child.
8. Work that inhibits the child's self esteem.[7]

It is beyond the shade of doubt that politically, socially and economically child is the need of future. Child is not only the future of a nation and its aspirations but also, and mainly, its strength in reserve. The future of a nation is best insured if its children are healthy and active, educated and informed, disciplined and trained, as well as free from social prejudices and above all having a scientific outlook.

The problem of child labour is not a concomitant feature of modern society only; in fact the problem has been there since the very dawn of human civilization. The reasons responsible for this phenomenon are varied and have been changing as the years rolled on. Avenues of child labour over the years have broadened. As a matter of fact, the problem is vexed and widespread and is not a characteristic feature of any particular type of economy. It is prevalent even in highly advanced countries of the world, though in a disguised form.

General Definitions

A *child* is defined as an individual under the age of 18 years, based on the 1989 United Nations Convention on the Rights of the Child and the ILO Convention on the Worst Forms of Child Labour, 1999 (No. 182). Since it is commonly accepted that a child under 5 years of age is too young to be engaged in work (although there are cases of exploitation or abuse by adults) or to start schooling,[8] we considered only the child population aged 5-17 years for the purpose of our estimates.

Working Children

Work is defined in terms of economic activity in the sense of the System of National Accounts (SNA) 1993.[9] This corresponds to the international definition of employment as adopted by the Thirteenth International Conference of Labour Statisticians.[10]

Economic activity covers all market production (paid work) and certain types of non-market production (unpaid work), including production of goods for own use. Whether paid or unpaid, therefore, the activity or occupation could be pursued in either the formal or informal sector and in either urban or rural areas. For example, children engaged in unpaid activities in a market-oriented establishment operated by a relative living in the same household are considered as working in an economic activity. Children working as maids or other domestic workers in someone else's household are also considered economically active. Children engaged in domestic chores within their own household, however, are not classified as economically active.[11]

In line with the international definition of employment, one hour of work during the reference week is sufficient to consider a person as being at work in economic activity during that week. Also included in the classification are individuals with a job but who are temporarily absent from work due to illness, vacation, or other reasons.

Note that the concept of "working children" based on economic activity excludes children seeking work or those who are currently unemployed.[12]

Child Labour

Not all work performed by children is equivalent to "child labour" needing abolition. Work in the sense of 'economic activity', is a statistical definition:

- Acceptable form of work by children (which may be regarded as positive), on the one hand, and child labour that needs to be eliminated, on the other,[13] and between

- Various forms of child labour and the WFCL, which require urgent action for elimination.

A Brief History of Child Labour

Although "child labour" as a social issue emerged as a consequence of the industrial revolution, children have always worked. They carried out tasks in the home, participated in agriculture, and learned crafts from an early age. This activity was taken for granted, and there were no debates over whether children should play a role in the economy.[14]

All of this changed with the recruitment of children for industrial production beginning with Britain in the eighteenth century. The situation of children in British mines and textile mills was the target of several parliamentary investigations in the early nineteenth century, and the plight of youthful chimney sweeps young children who cleaned the inside of coal burning chimneys, in the process acquiring serious respiratory diseases, challenged the conscience of the country.

Over time, legislation was introduced which gradually outlawed many of these activities, beginning with the introduction of Half-Time Working in conjunction with the Factory Acts of 1833 and 1844. The purpose behind this system was to restructure child labour so that it no longer interfered with education (Hobbs and McKechnic, 1997). Beginning with the Education Act of 1918, regulation sought the removal of all younger children from the labour force; this approach was extended by the Young Person's Act 1933, which embodied the modern approach of age limits and hazardous orders.

Nevertheless, there has been a debate surrounding how consequential these legislative actions really were. On the one hand, many children continued to engage in economic activities prohibited under law, and inspectors either failed to recognise infractions or they turned a blind eye to them (Hobbs and McKechnie, 1997). On the other, while the prevalence of child labour in Britain certainly declined over the span of the nineteenth and twentieth centuries, many scholars have tended to downplay the role played by legislation compared with other changes in society. Some, such as Fyfe, believe that the increasing availability of education and the greater importance attached to it by most British families, was the primary factor at work. In most cases, agitation and action by politicians and trade unionists and also by some entrepreneurs has lead to legislative and concrete action to reduce the incidence of child labour during the closing decade of the 19th century and the early decades of the 20th century.[15] Others such as Nardenelli, hold that rising family income encouraged families to withhold their children's labour (Nardinelli, 1990). Unravelling these factors is difficult since they were contemporaneous and deeply interrelated. The British experience was echoed by other industrialized countries, although each has a distinctive history (Cunningham and Viazzo, 1996).[16]

Early years of industrialization were accompanied by an important role for children in the factory workforce, although in some countries, such as Japan, this participation was muted by the cultural value attached to children's freedom to play.

Eventually, public concern for the welfare of the children was aroused and protective legislation enacted. The parallel forces of emerging mass education and rising incomes also played their part. To some extent, all of these countries have tended to converge on a new pattern of youthful employment. Although the problems of the past have not been fully eradicated, it is fair to say that, until recently, public opinion in most of the developed countries regarded child labour as a topic for the history books, and there was no systematic attempt to monitor the economic activity of children.[17]

So far as the origin of child labour in India is concerned, it has its roots in two traditions—(i) from children learning their disciplines and skills of work from their parents; and (ii) from bonded labour where a young child is given to a landlord in lieu of debt repayment and the landlord uses him or her as his bonded servant. Vagrant and illegal trades also attract a few youngsters as easy money through low wages makes their life temporarily comfortable. Besides this, urbanization, rapid industrialization and growing unemployment amongst adults, too have a contributory effect on the employment of children.[18]

In Kautilya's Arthshastra, there is also a mention of employment of children in India in the form of slavery. During this period (3rd century B.C.) child slaves, who were less than eight years of age, were known to be working in many nobles' houses. During the medieval period there were certain crafts which totally depended on the employment of children. As such, children were normally placed as trainees under artisans and craftsman. Even now this tradition continues especially in carpet, cotton and silk weaving industries. These industries employ a large number of children to perform various activities related to these industries.[19]

The phenomenon of child labour was prevalent all over the world, in the pre-industrial revolution phase, though it had an altogether different nature and magnitude. During the post industrial revolution phase, child labour became a growing phenomenon upto the first half of this century in industrialized countries. In case of developing countries, it still continues to grow. With the economic recession, this problem was expected to become more acute. It has started making its appearance in industrialized countries. It is also witnessed in the third world, in general and in India in particular, as a result of persistent poverty and the population explosion.[20]

However, now the nature and magnitude of the problem of child labour is largely different. But in case of India, some of the past characteristics of the problem are still present. Although, all over the world, children are exploited through wage employment and self-employment, still almost nowhere else does this problem feature so high in the priority of government and non-governmental organizations.[21]

Rapid urbanization has made the problem of child labour more visible because of its association with work outside the family context and high rate of rural-urban migration of both the family and individual types. In case of a developing country like India, we find that the children mainly work in small manufacturing units as cheap labour. We also find that due to technical innovations in the urban sector, children are often forced into street trades turning child labour into casual labour.[22]

Thus we see that child labour has existed in one form or the other in all historical times. However, a significant change that has taken place is its hazardous nature and graver magnitude that has made its perception as a social problem.

Child Labour at the Global Level

Child labour is a pervasive problem throughout the world. Industrialized economies especially of Europe, North America, and

Australia etc. have by now reduced employment of children to a considerable extent; they are yet not fully out of the phenomenon of child labour. Some of them have some child labour originated from social problems, educational systems and poverty. But the problem of child labour as faced by developing economies today has indeed serious dimensions Africa and Asia together account for over ninety per cent of total child employment. Though there are more child workers in Asia than anywhere else, a higher percentage of African children participate in the labour force.

It is clear that there are more children as a percentage of the total child population working in the developing countries than in the industrialized ones. They start work at a younger age, sometimes but not always within the family home. The variety of jobs they do is greater than in the developed countries, and less recognised by the authorities. They enjoy fewer legal or other protections, if any, and no training to help them deal with the health and other hazards of their work, and they are often helpless to counter poor treatment and exploitation by their employers (or by their families). All in all, children in developing countries work much harder than those in industrialized countries, for less reward and most often foregoing the benefits of schooling. Some even have to create their own jobs, which they do by working on the streets or scavenging for garbage.

The young workers in the developed countries are in a better position. Perhaps their biggest advantage is that many of them manage to combine work with schooling, and one reason for this is the heavy emphasis on school attendance by the local authorities. Child labour remains one of the most neglected human rights issues of our time. Child labour is the major cause of child abuse and exploitation in many parts of the world. No one knows for certain how many children are working. Africa has the highest proportion in the world of working children (nearly one third), whilst Latin America, with its high levels of urbanization, has the largest population of "street children". And in many Asian countries children comprise over ten per cent of the work force. Yet it is remarkably persistent and remains widespread in much of the developing world, including in the booming parts of the world economy. A 2003 survey by the International Labour Organization (ILO) suggested that there are 246 million child labourers (aged 14 years or less) in the world and that as many as 180 million of them are engaged in hazardous activities that put them at direct physical risk.

Within this, it is generally accepted that India has the largest number of child labourers in the world. The United Nations Children's Fund (UNICEF) estimates that there are more than thirty five million such children, accounting for fourteen per cent of the children in the five to fourteen years age group. Other unofficial estimates are much higher, ranging between 60 and 125 million child labourers. Mean while, the census data for 2001 suggests a much lower incidence, with 12.5 million child labourers identified, which would be less than five per cent of the relevant age group. This represents a declining incidence compared with the 1991 figure of 6.4 per cent of the children between five and fourteen years. Out of the total population of child labourers in India females constitute 46.26 per cent whereas male child labourers made it 53.74 per cent.

Trends in Children's Work[23]

The Table 1.1 and 1.2 shows, incidence of work among children.

Sectoral Distribution of Children's Work

The indicator for employment by sector-based on the International Standard Industrial Classification of All Economic Activities, Revisions 2 (1968) and 3 (1990)-breaks employment down into three broad groupings of economic activity: agriculture, industry, and services.*

- The agricultural sector comprises activities in agriculture, hunting, forestry, and fishing. Children's work is primarily concentrated in agriculture-as Chart below illustrates, agriculture accounts for more than two-thirds (69 per cent) of all working children in the age group 5 to 14.

---

* *Note*: this is the first time that ILO is in a position to present reliable estimates on the sectoral distribution of working children. There are therefore no benchmark 2000 data with which these results can be compared. Moreover, data presented is for children's work only. The existing data material did not allow us to analyze sect oral data on the more specific groups of children in child labour and hazardous work.

Table 1.1: Estimates of Various Forms of Children's Work, 2000 and 2004

Age Group		*Child Population* 2000	*Child Population* 2004	*Working Children* 2000	*Working Children* 2004	*Child Labourers* 2000	*Child Labourers* 2004	*Children in Hazardous Work* 2000	*Children in Hazardous Work* 2004
5-17	No. (millions)	1531.4	1566.3	351.9	317.4	245.5	217.7	170.5	126.3
	Incidence (Percentage of age group)	100.0	100.0	23.0	20.3	16.0	13.9	11.1	8.1
	Percentage change from 2000 to 2004	—	2.3	—	–9.8	—	–11.3	—	–25.9
5-14	No. (million)	1199.4	1206.5	211.0	190.7	186.3	165.8	111.3	74.4
	Incidence (Percentage of age group)	100.0	100.0	17.6	15.8	15.5	13.7	9.3	6.2
	Percentage change from 2000 to 2004	—	0.6	—	–9.6	—	–11.0	—	–33.2
15-17	No. (million)	332.0	359.8	140.9	126.7	59.2	51.9	59.2	51.9
	Incidence (Percentage of age group)	100.0	100.0	42.4	35.2	17.8	14.4	17.8	14.4
	Percentage change from 2000 to 2004	—	8.4	—	–10.1	—	–12.3	—	–12.3

Source: International Labour Office. 2006. *Global Child Labour Trends 2000 to 2004*. Geneva: ILO.

Table 1.2: Regional Trends in Children's Work, 2000-2004 (5 to 14 Years Olds)

Region	*Child Population (Million)*		*Economically Active Children (Million)*		*Activity Rate (%)*	
	2000	2004	2000	2004	2000	2004
Asia and the Pacific	655.1	650.0	127.3	122.3	19.4	18.8
Latin America and the Caribbean	108.1	111.0	17.4	5.7	16.1	5.1
Sub-Saharan Africa	166.8	186.8	48.0	49.3	28.8	26.4
Other regions	269.3	258.8	18.3	13.4	6.8	5.2
World	1,199.3	1,206.6	211.0	190.7	17.6	15.8

Source: International Labour Office. *2006. Global Child Labour Trends 2000 to 2004.* Geneva: ILO.

- The industry sector comprises mining and quarrying, manufacturing, construction, and public utilities (electricity, gas and water). Industry accounts for 9 per cent of working children.
- The services sector consists of wholesale and retail trade; restaurants and hotels; transport, storage, and communications; finance, insurance, real-estate, and business services; and community as well as social personal services. Services account for 22 per cent of working children.

Chart. 1.1: Working Children Ages 5-14 by Sector (%)

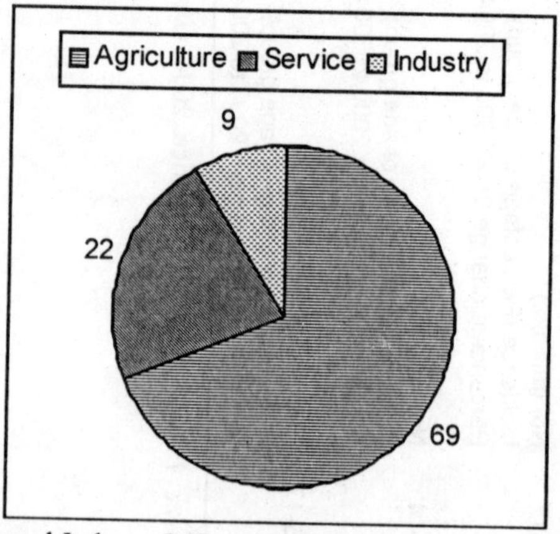

Source: International Labour Office. 2006. *Global Child Labour Trends 2000 to 2004*. Geneva: ILO.

Human Rights Perspective and Legal Framework of Child Labour

Human rights were formally acknowledged and declared in realization of the need to safeguard and promote the inherent dignity of all members of human society. Prior to the Convention on the Rights of the Child, human rights standards applicable to all members of the human family had been expressed in legal instruments such as covenants, conventions and declarations. By, 1989, the standards concerning children were brought together in a single legal instrument agreed to by the international community. It unambiguously spelt out the rights to which every child is entitled, regardless of place of birth, descent, sex, religion, or social origin.[24]

Convention on the Rights of the Child

The General Assembly of the United Nations adopted the Convention on the Rights of the Child (CRC) on 20th November 1989. It bears the opinion regarding protection of children everywhere against exploitation, neglect and abuse. The Convention draws attention four sets of civil, political, social, economic and cultural rights of every child. These include (1) The Right to Survival; (2) The Right to Protection; (3) The Right to Development; and (4) The Right to Participation. Article 23 of the Convention says, 'All States should work to end such child labour practices and see how the conditions and circumstances of children in legitimate employment can be protected to provide adequate opportunity for their healthy upbringing and development.[25]

World Conference on Human Rights

The World Conference on Human Rights organized by the U.N.O., which was held in Veina, Austria from 14th to 25th June 1993 deeply, concerned the rights of Children in global society. The conference reiterated the principle of "First Call for Children"[26] and, in this respect it underlined the importance of major national and international efforts, especially those of the United Nations Children's Emergency Fund (UNICEF), for promoting respect for the rights of the child to survival, protection, development and participation. It called on states to integrate the Convention on the Rights of the child into their National Action Plans.[27]

The World Conference on Human Rights urged all states, with the support of international cooperation, to address the acute problem of children under difficult circumstances. Exploitation and abuse of children should be actively combated, by addressing their root causes. Effective measures are required against harmful child labour. The conference supported all measures by the United Nations and its specialized agencies to ensure the effective protection and promotion of human rights of the female child. It urged states to respect existing laws and regulations and remove customs and practices, which discriminate against and cause harm to the female child. It recognized the important role played by NGOs in the effective implementation of all human rights instruments and, in particular, the Convention on the Rights of the Child (Veina Declaration and Programme of Action, 1993).[28]

As early as 1921, when the International Labour Organization (ILO) passed the first Minimum Age Convention, the world has attempted to protect children's right to an education and to prevent any child labour which would prejudice their school attendance.[29] The ILOs Minimum Age Convention 138 of 1973[30] set the standard for the minimum age for admission to employment as 15 years, or in special cases where economic and educational facilities are insufficiently developed, 14 years; light work not harmful to the child or prejudicial to his or her attendance at school is permissibly after age 12. Since 1990, with the entry into force of the Convention on the Rights of the Child,[31] the child's right to be protected from "any work that is likely to be hazardous or to interfere with the child's education" (Article 32) and his or her right, on an equal, non-discriminatory basis to "primary education compulsory and available free to all" (Article 28) have gained the status of internationally recognized norms, while imposing an obligation on the 192 states parties to the Convention to realize these rights for the children under their jurisdiction.[32] In 2000, children were provided further protection through the entry into force of ILO Convention 182,[33] which was ratified by 150 countries as of May 2004.[34] Convention 182 prohibits the worst forms of child labour, defined as all forms of slavery and similar practices; child prostitution and pornography; illicit activities (in particular the production and trafficking of drugs); and work that is likely to harm the health, safety or morals of children.[35]

The Geneva declaration of the Rights of the Child 1924 was the first convention of League of Nations to discuss the rights of child.[36] The Universal Declaration of Human Rights as adopted by the United Nations in 1948, incorporate the basic rights of children for growth and education. An independent "Declaration on the Rights of child" was made by United Nations in 1959.[37] This emphasized on special protection and care for child to develop in a normal and healthy manner in an atmosphere of freedom and dignity.

The United Nations Declarations emphasized on child welfare having applications to every social condition, by conferring specific rights to children through social legislation prohibiting any discrimination.[38] The year 1979,[39] was designated as International Year of the Child (IYC) by United Nations which gave importance on the co-operation of the Nations in common tasks of meeting the basic needs of the children, i.e. nutrition, health, education, maternal protection, family care, equal society status and protection from racial and other forms of discrimination.[40] This was a challenge to the conscience of mankind and to the community of nations.

On November 20, 1989, the General Assembly of the United Nations adopted a Convention of Rights of the Child which was ratified by 107 member countries within a year and India was a signatory to it. The convention contains 54 articles, each dealing with different types of rights. These can be broken down into four broad categories such as-survival rights, developing rights, protection right and participation rights.[41] Several rights cover a child's right to the life and the basic need for existence which include adequate living standard, shelter, nutrition and access to medical services. Developing rights include the aspects those held children to reach their fullest potential, such as, rights to education, play and leisure, culture activities, access to information, and freedom of thought conscience and religion. Protection right require the children be safeguarded against all forms of abuse, neglect and exploitation which include child labour, drug abuse, sexual exploitation, abuses in criminal justice system, etc. Protection right allow children to take an active role in their communities and nations. These encompass the freedom of expression, to join associations and to assemble peacefully which is necessary for preparation of a complete and responsible adulthood.[42]

In, 1919, International Labour Organization, in its first session adopted a convention on minimum age of children for admission into industrial employment. It laid down that no child under 14 should be employed in any public or private undertaking other than in which only family members are employed.[43] Industrial undertaking, here include mines, queries, manufacturing units, construction, maintenance and repairs and transportation of passengers and goods by road, rail or in water way. The minimum age was revised from 14 to 15 in the Convention No. 59 of 1973. The Convention which grew out of the personal initiative of the Director-General Wilfred Jenks[44], marks important progress in raising the standard for general employment in developed countries from 14 years (accepted during the first reading in 1972) to 15 years, or the age at which compulsory education ended, whichever was the higher (accepted in 1973).[45] Subsequently ILO, prohibited employment of children in agriculture undertaking, shops, hotels, restaurants, offices, places of public employment, etc. ratified all its conventions. The Convention No. 138 of 1973 of ILO emphasized that each member for which the convention was in force undertakes to pursue a national goal designed to ensure the effective abolition of child labour and to raise regressively the minimum age for admission of children to employment of work. The same convention also recommended for special attention for working conditions of young persons below 18 years, in terms of fair remuneration, limited working hours, prohibited night work, weekly and annual holidays with leave, coverage by all social schemes, maintenance of satisfactory standards of health, safety, etc.

ILO has adopted five conventions for making medical examination of young persons, a condition precedent for employment. This is to ensure fitness of the young persons for the employment where he/she is to be employed.[46]

Also, three conventions were made in support of prohibition of night work of young persons both in industrial and non-industrial establishments. However, ILO, through various conventions and recommendations made rules and guided the member countries for abolition of child labour through various measures.

Constitutional Safeguards in India

The constitution of India carries important expression of the attitude of the State towards children, Article-15 (3) of the constitution authorizes the state for the making of any special provision for women and children. Article-24 provides that no child below the age of 14 shall be employed to work in any factory or mine or engaged in any other hazardous employment. Article 39 (E) proclaims that the State shall ensure its policy towards securing, that the health strengths of the tender age of children are not forced by economic necessity to enter vocations unsuited to their age or strength. Article 39 (E) enjoins that childhood and youth are to be protected against exploitation, against moral and material abandonment. In Article-45 the constitution also endeavours to provide free and compulsory education for all children until they complete the age of 14 years.[47]

The general provisions under Article, 38, 42, 43, 45 and 47 of Directive Principles of State Policy, although do not deal directly with child welfare but provides strategy for indirectly promoting welfare of children.

Article-38(1) provides that the State shall strive to promote the welfare of the people by securing and protecting as effectively, as it may secure a social order in which justice, social, economic and political shall be ensured.

Article-42 and 43 provide for securing just and human conditions of work and hold out a promise that the State shall endeavour to secure, by suitable legislation, economic organization or in any other way, for all workers, a living wage with specified conditions of work ensuring a decent standard of life and full employment of leisure and social and culture opportunities. This definitely includes child labourers in widest sense. [48]

Article-46 makes provisions for promotion, with special care of the educational and economic interest of SC and STs and other weaker sections of the society. Article-47 lays emphasis on raising standard of living of people by the State. These also include children in their purview.

While assessing the progress and implementation of these provisions, it is disappointing to note that child labour exploitation is rampant in all spheres and increasing day by day. For this responsibility does not lie exclusively with the State but with parents and children. Parents consider sending children for education brings double loss by them. Also, the problem is so complex that it involves many social and economic factors. Unless they are taken care of, the problem is difficult to be solved.

Legal Measures for Protection of Child Labour

The Factories Act of 1881 was the first law to define child and to prescribe prohibitory regulations for employment of children below 7 years of age. The Factories Act, 1911 prohibited employment of children in dangerous occupations and working during night hours. The first Convention of ILO, compelled amendment of the Act in 1922, to raise the minimum age of child to 15 years. However, children below the age of 12 years where prohibited for employment. The age raised to 13 years in 1935 under the Act. The present Factories Act, 1948, prescribes prohibitory regulations for employment of children below 14 years of age in any factory. India Mines Act, 1951 prohibits employment of children below 16 years in any underground mines. But Plantation Labour Act, 1951 has prescribed this age as 12 years. The Motor Transport Workers Act 1961 absolutely prohibits employment of children in it. The Shops and Commercial Establishments Acts of different States, also prohibit employment of children in the shops and commercial establishments.

These legislations are also careful about the health of young persons to be employed. While restricting the night work, they provides for medical fitness certificates by the young persons. They also clarify about the conditions where they are to be employed. Of course, in many cases deliberate violations of the provisions take place either by the medical practitioners or employers. Also, the parents who satisfy their economic needs lie about the age of their children.

Besides the above legislations, The Apprentice Act, 1961, The Beedi and Cigar Workers (Conditions of Employment) Act, 1966, The Atomic Energy Act, 1962 and Contract Labour (Regulation and Abolition) Act, 1970 provide Prohibitory and Regularity measures for employment of children.

As required by ILO Convention and as envisaged in National

Seminar on Employment of Children in 1975, to prevent exploitation of children, Indian Government felt to enact a single Act to deal with prohibition of child labour. The Gurupadaswamy Report of 1979, also emphasized on such a comprehensive law for the purpose. As a result, the Child Labour (Prohibition and Regulation) Act was enacted in 1986.

The Act prohibited employment of children below the age of 14 years in certain occupations and processes. These include the transport of passengers, goods and mails and other hazardous work in railways and ports, the process like Beedi making, cement manufacturing, manufacturing of matches and explosives, mica cutting, soap manufacturing, wool cleaning and building and construction industries.

The 3rd part of the Act provides for regulations of conditions of work by prescribing minimum working hours, prohibiting work at night, prohibiting overtime work, and weekly holiday. Also, the Act provides measures for health and safety of child workers. It emphasized on maintenance of a register having details of children if employed by any organization.

While prohibiting employment in certain occupation and processes, the law legalized employment of children in other cases. Indirect support was extended for such an evil practice which should be totally prohibited irrespective of the nature of employment.

Education and Child Labour

While education itself is clearly significant for the development of an individual and for the well being of the society, it may be less obvious why education is important in the context of child labour. How are the two linked? Does child labour have an impact on children's school attendance? Can education play a role in combating child labour? If so, how it can be improved? These questions will be dealt with in this section.

Over 70 million primary school aged children, and a much larger number of secondary school aged children, are not enrolled in school. Many more children are enrolled in school but do not attend regularly. Most of these children are among the world's child labourers.[49]

Widespread child labour is closely associated with poverty. The family may depend on the contribution a working child makes to the household income, and place more importance on that income than on education. A poor family may be unable to afford school fees, uniforms or other costs. Moreover, when a family has to make a choice between sending either a boy or girl to school, it is often the girl who loses out.

A child who is full time in school is more likely not to engage in child labour. Hence, expanding access to free and compulsory education is crucial to reducing child labour, as is the provision of quality education. Access to education is a necessary but not sufficient element as the challenge is to retain children in school. Only quality education can ensure that they stay in school. Quality means that teachers are recruited in adequate numbers to avoid high student teacher ratios in classrooms. Teachers and educators need to receive the training required to make them effective. Relevant curricula are also essential for an education of quality. Finally, no good education can be provided if classroom conditions are deplorable and students lack the necessary books, equipment and other educational materials. Children who receive an education of quality are more empowered to escape from poverty and, as adults, are more likely to send their children to school.[50]

Attending school in the morning and studying at home in the afternoon require time and so does working. Depending on the circumstances, it may be difficult for a child to find enough hours during the day to combine the two. A child's work can also compete with schooling in terms of money. While child labour is often a much needed contribution to the income of the family, education may be so costly that the decision whether to send a child to school or to work will be difficult for many poor parents.

Kanbargi and Kulkarni have examined the interrelation between child work, schooling and fertility in rural Karnataka. The study found a significant inverse relation between child labour and child schooling at the micro level. While the age of the child and the presence of younger siblings at home determined child labour, the age of the child and education of the father determined the schooling of children. However the study did not find any direct relationship between child labour and fertility; child labour significantly affects fertility through its negative effect on schooling. Since schooling had a negative effect on fertility, the overall effect of child labour on fertility was found to be positive. The analysis suggests that a reduction in the incidence of child labour and an increase in child schooling would lead to a decline in fertility.[51]

Child Labour and School Achievement

Myron Wiener and others hold the view argued that the universal extension of state-funded education in Europe, North America and Japan has been the most powerful instrument for the abolition of child labour. "No country has successfully ended child labour without first making education compulsory. As long as children need not attend school, they will enter the labour force". Policy makers in most countries believe that mandatory education is a prerequisite for the eventual abolition of all forms of child labour.[52] Wiener also conclude in his book that child labour prevails due to illiteracy and refuted the popularly accepted explanations given by scholars on child labour, viz., low economic development of the nation, poverty, high birth rate and size of family.[53]

The expected returns to education (i.e. the benefits relative to the cost of education) are an important factor in the parents' considerations. However, the true benefits of schooling, such as increased future wages may often not be known to families, and even if they are, weighing up value against private costs is not an easy task. Even if parents are aware that the returns to education could be significant, the cost of schooling can be so high that the children are removed from school and pushed into works.[54] The benefits of going to school are mostly long-term, and will mainly affect the child, rather than the parent. On the other hand, the costs have to be born by the parents, and these costs are due in the short term. A comparative study of child labour and schooling in Africa found that one way to reduce child labour and increase incentives to keep the children in the educational system is to improve access to credit, which the family can pay back later. [55]

Education of good quality is a key element in the prevention of child labour. Children with no access to education have little alternative than to enter the labour market. Child labour is also one of the main obstacles to education for all, since children who are working full-time cannot go to school. The academic achievement of children who combine work and school often suffers, and there is a strong tendency for these children to drop out of school and enter into full-time employment.

When education is compulsory and attractive, it can help to reduce child labour. There is need to develop an integrated policy and programme of action to provide quality free and universal education that is relevant and accessible to children in poor families such as those to which the majority of child workers belong. Child labour concerns should be explicitly addressed and integrated into such a policy and programme of action; a holistic approach is necessary. Quality education should be provided for children at least upto 15 years of age to stem the flow of children into the labour market and to provide working children and former working children with educational opportunities. A recent study estimates that worldwide an additional US$ 16 billion dollar per year would be required to achieve universal primary education of decent quality by 2015 (Matz, 2003).[56]

Table 1.3: Annual Expenditure on Basic Education and Other Items

S. No.	*The World's Priorities (Annual Expenditure)*	*US$*
1.	Basic Education	6 bn
2.	Ice Cream in Europe	11 bn
3.	Perfumes in Europe and USA	12 bn
4.	Pet foods in Europe and USA	17 bn
5.	Business entertainment in Japan	35 bn
6.	Cigarettes in Europe	50 bn
7.	Alcoholic drinks in Europe	105 bn
8.	Narcotic drugs in the world	400 bn
9.	Military spending in the world	780 bn

Source: UNDP, Human Development Report 1998.

This table indicates that the world can surely afford to invest more money in the well-being of its children. However, while universal access to education is affordable in global terms, there are many countries, particularly in Africa, for which the costs of financing the types of education programmes described in this section are too high. These countries must rely on increased donor assistance from the developed countries to meet the present educational challenges.

NGOs can play an important role in this regard. No other suggestion is as important as the linking of education with the individual's life, need and ambitions so as to make him a powerful instrument of social, economic and cultural transformation, and to fulfil national objectives through him. This is possible only when education is linked with productivity. Simultaneously it could develop truly indigenous life style that could go with modernization. Above all education could develop a sense of cooperation and could formulate a character through stress on social, moral and spiritual values.[57]

Child Labour and Gender

In all societies, boys and girls are assigned different societal roles and experience different perspectives of life as a result of their being male or female. Such differences have an immense impact on their lives. The importance of gender perspective is very important in understanding the complexity of child labour. Gender, as opposed to sex, refers to the social differences and relations between boys and girls that are learned and vary widely within and between cultures and change over time. Sex refers to biological differences between boys and girls, men and women. They are universal and do not change.

For many years, policies, studies and programmes dealing with child labour have focused on boys, under the assumption that their needs and perspectives were identical to that of girls. As a result, girl child labourers were often made invisible whereas they represent a very large proportion of working children. It is only recently that working girls have received increased attention largely due to the historic Convention on the Rights of the Child, the commitments adopted during the Fourth World Conference on Women (1995).[58]

The issue of gender is now universally regarded as a vital component in addressing child labour. Although they are exposed to many similar types of labour as boys, girls often endure additional hardships and are more susceptible to exploitation, sometimes as a result of their society's view of the role women and girls should play. Of particular concern is the fact that often constitutes a large proportion of the children involved in some of the worst forms of child labour, namely commercial sexual exploitation.

For girls in particular, there are factors that create a conflict between child labour and education, and they are clearly reflected in the large gender gaps in schooling: sixty per cent of the children around the world who do not go to school are girls. Girls' education is threatened in many countries by the frequent preference for educating sons, by early marriage, and by inheritance and social security laws that disadvantage women. Other factors that limit girls' educational opportunities range from the distance to schools, which place their security at risk, to the provision of relevant curricula sensitive to their needs and aspirations. In certain cultures, a girl's chances of going to school might depend on the availability of separate school facilities for girls (who cannot for cultural or religious reasons sit in the same schoolrooms with boys) or the presence of a female teacher. These and other problems often deprive millions of girls of an education.[59]

The value of girls' work and the high opportunity cost of foregoing it, poor opportunities for skilled employment after obtaining an education, and the prescribed role of girls who are expected anyway to have a life of domesticity and subservience are all confounding factors. Their education appears as a poor investment for many parents. Often, when faced with limited resources and many financial demands, parents prefer to invest in the education of their sons and not lose their daughters' critical contribution to the household economy.[60] There is a need of gender sensitive education. Child labour has an impact on different cultures and individuals in a variety of ways. Education concerning child labour should be both comprehensive and tailored to reach a variety of target audiences.

Although gender perspectives continue to appear more frequently in analysis of child labour, there is still a lot of work to be done in grasping the role gender plays in determining the various forms and the extent of child labour.

There is no denying the fact that both girls and boys engage in the worst forms of child labour. However, it is important to realize that due to certain societal expectations, duties and responsibilities placed on girls, they are often more vulnerable to exploitation. Thus, the different expectations that society places on girls, as well as the differences in their situations and conditions must be taken into account before taking protective action. It is to understand the virtual culture and environment in which child labour occurs in order to address all of the root causes of child labour, including gender bias.

Surveys published by ILO reveal that the total number of working children increased dramatically, and working girls out numbered working boys. From 1981 there is an increase in the work participation rate of girls and a decrease in the case of boys.[61]

The problem of female child labour is a highly complex one. From birth to graveyard, female children toil hard both in and outside the family. Young female children of school age going to industries as a worker are on the increase. Patriarchal society has deeply internalized the idea of male supremacy and female dependency. Consciously or unconsciously our society, has been reinforcing the stereotypes of gender roles and expectations, with the result that girls find it almost impossible to break out of the mould that is cast for them by society. The female children are marred by neglects, discrimination, lack of opportunities and limited life options.[62]

Gender discrimination often results in disparity in girls' enrolment, high dropout rate and their early involvement in economic activities. The female child helps the family to survive by spending her time and in this process she misses out education, good nutrition and future employment avenues that may be remunerative. Case studies about the children in employment reflect the pathetic plight of these children, particularly girls who suffer much more than boys.

The predominance of female labourers is reflected in the findings of various studies conducted in the garment industry in India, match, fireworks and beedi industries in Tamilnadu or in the bangle industry in Ferozabad. The findings showed that fifty to eighty per cent of them lost their childhood, struggling between her work place and domestic chores at home. Female children are exploited unmercifully in many industries. Sometimes sexual abuse is also inflicted upon them. The crux of the problem of the female child is that she is caught in a situation, in which she cannot change, which is predetermined, pre-cast and pre-destined. Society has already defined her role, which is based on a male view. The societal preference for male children result in girls being valued less, fed less, educated less but worked harder and deprived of every opportunity to broaden their personal, social and intellectual horizons. In certain communities, the rules of permission and restriction on women and female children are much more stringent which allow for greater exploitation and discrimination.[63]

Culture of Exploiting Women and Female Children

In most of the developing countries even today, the female child has a lower status and enjoys fewer childhood rights, opportunities, and benefits than the male child who has the first call on family and community resources. With the female child begins the process of inequality that the adult woman finds so difficult to overcome. Even where poverty is not an overriding factor in childhood development, gender inhibits equal opportunities for girls.

Family preferences tend to favour boys over girls; family decisions in the distribution of food, labour, health care, and access to schooling and other life changing opportunities usually benefit boys more than girls. A real gender differential in children is rooted in cultural perception. Available evidence indicates the pride with which a newborn male child is welcomed and cynicism that greet the baby girl.[64]

Female children work in large numbers and for long hours in and outside the household, but their labour is unacknowledged or under-represented in formal labour statistics. Parental perception also contributes to the underrating of the labour of the female child. Such attitudes explain why boys are often given greater opportunities to learn economically valuable skills than girls.

Gender disparity in education is influenced by the lack of educational facilities and cultural norms, which hold that girls are only 'born to marry' and, therefore, addressing the needs of the female child could be the key to achieving a more equitable status and meaningful role for women in the long run.[65]

Gender may influence child labour in ways similar to age. The returns to education may vary with gender. This seems likely to be especially important in third world where men and women participate in different economic activities. Likewise, the returns to activities other then age may also vary across genders because of discrimination of the sex typing of tasks. Moreover age and gender may interact in important ways. First, girls develop earlier than boys so they may be capable of more sophisticated tasks at certain age. As puberty onsets, boys may develop comparative advantage in more physical activities. Second, the sex typing of tasks may be more important in the types of activities performed by older children. Hence gender difference in household or market work may manifest itself both in the types of activities performed at a given age, and these gender differences may vary with age. The research shows that the largest gender differences are in household production, and these gender differences are increasing in age.[66]

Globalization and Child Labour

The process of international integration of economic activities through liberalizing international trade has pushed more workers into the informal sector of both developing and developed countries. In the developing countries, more than in the developed countries, this has led to the economic exploitation of children in the production of goods both for the export and the domestic market. According to the International Labour Organization (ILO), more children are possibly involved in the urban informal sector than in the agricultural sector, because of fast growing migration into the cities and the decentralization of production units.

One of the recent research shows that children are less likely to work in countries with more international trade. The negative association between trade and child labour holds even when considering only poor countries' trade with high-income countries. It also holds up for trade in unskilled-labour intensive products. Quite simply, child labour is less prevalent in countries that trade more because countries that trade more are richer, and children work less in richer countries. Yet, child involvement in the production of products for export is not evidence that the export opportunity causes children to work. (Eric Edmonds, 2007).

Some economists and social scientists perceive that globalization increases child labour and marshals several reasons for this. They argue that decentralized production process and intensified competition over wage costs leads to an increase in the number of employed children. Secondly, the weakening of trade unions has also result in falling of real wage of workers and the absence of alternative gainful employment children are pushed to the workplace at tender age. Some on the basis of cross-country empirical investigations argue that globalization does not necessarily increase child labour. Either it reduces or at best has no significant effect on child labour. This is so as globalization process increases the real wage rate of largely uneducated workforce relatively to the educated workers. The increase in real wages makes the poorer families less poor and enables them to finance the investment on education of their children and thereby complements the other ongoing effect, aimed at combating the problem of child labour. Thus for a developing country, with large uneducated force, trade expansion seems to help in reducing child labour. The last group of opinion makers takes an electric position by saying that the relationship between trade and child labour depends upon the type of activities in which a country specializes, and the macro economic policies it pursues. (Triloknath Mishra, 2006, p. 60).

Globalization and Decrease in Child Labour

The study by (Alessandro Cigno, Furio C. Rosati and Lorenzo Guarcello, 1992)[67] has indicated that there is no empirical evidence that indicate trade exposure *per se* increases child labour. As trade theory and household economics lead us to expect, cross-country evidence seems to indicate that trade reduces or, at worst, has no significant effect on child labour. Consistent with the theory, a comparatively well educated labour force and active social policy, appears to be conducive to a reduction in child labour. For countries with a largely uneducated workforce, the problem is not so much globalization, but mostly ineffective social mobilization and economic resources. The study has indicated that higher foreign trade between countries appears to be associated with a lower incidence of child labour.[68]

A clearly negative association between trade openness and child labour is evident only for Africa and Latin America. In Asia, the relationship between trade and child labour is much weaker (especially if the later is measured as a complement to the school enrolment rate).[69] This seems to indicate that the type of activity in which a country specializes, and the policies it pursues, shift the relationship between child labour and globalization. There is, therefore, no prima facie evidence that globalization will necessarily result in more child labour.

The argument is that the increased parental earnings may help parents reduce the work that children perform. Parents can buy substitutes for goods previously produced by children, or they can use their increased income to substitute for the money previously earned by children. A working child in the family, as a result of globalization, may provide incentives for other children in the family to stop working and attend schooling. Hence, globalization can help parents in poor countries to stop child labour without foreign intervention. A study conducted in Vietnam has suggested that when globalization improves the income of impoverished households, this additional income help parents reduce the workload of their children and send more of them to school.[70] If properly harnessed globalization should spur growth and economic development leading to social advance, including the elimination of child labour.

Globalization and Increase in Child Labour

However, other view point indicates that unfortunately, globalization is out of control and instead of reducing child labour it actually increases child labour, mainly in export industries. Although large scale manufacturing export industries in South and East Asian countries do not directly rely on child labour, but the backward linkages to these industries, through sub-contracting to labour intensive segments of the production of some of these export items like carpets, garments, rattan production of some of these export items like carpets, garments, rattan furniture, sports products (especially soccer balls), precious stones involve children from India, Bangladesh, Pakistan, Thailand, Philippines and Indonesia into limited indirect child labour use at the low-wage end of the production scale.[71] In 1999 and 2000, UNICEF interviewed children across 30 developing countries and discovered that factory work is rare. Only three percent of children worked outside their household for payment. Unpaid domestic work is more common than work for payment. UNICEF found that two percent of boys and five percent of girls perform unpaid domestic work for households other than their own. However, most working children are employed in their own households, helping with household duties or the family's farm or business.

It is also true that globalization increases a country's exposure to foreign competition. This may force inefficient firms in import-competing industries out of business. Regardless of the long-term benefits of this real location of resources, in the short-term, these adjustments may create difficulty for some households with children.

In case of such export industry child labour has little to do with poverty, culture or tradition. It is much more the result of greed, connivance and complacency. It is not at all surprising, especially when a child costs only one-sixth to one-third of the adult wage. The connivance of governments who turn a blind eye to the practice and in many cases enters into agreements with inward investors, where the concerned labour laws of the country can not be applied is distressful. The complacency of the society (all of us) who wants cheaper consumer products, regardless of the exploitation involved in production is the main cause of increase in child labour.[72]

Social scientists vary in how they view a parent's decision to send a child to work. The debate revolves around how parents in developing countries view child labour. In one view, parents want their children to work. Perhaps parents even have children in order to send the children to work.[73] This view implies that parents take advantage of any earning opportunity. So long as, parents benefit more when the child works than when the child goes to school, child labour will persist. Improvements in living standards may do nothing to ameliorate child labour. In such situations globalization is bound to increase child labour, if not regulated and monitored by the government and the civil society organizations.

The effects of globalization on child labour growth, due to the exports of carpets from India, garment manufacturing from Bangladesh, India and Honduras and sports especially soccer ball manufacturing from Pakistan are classic examples of linkages between globalization and child labour. This has been repeated all around the world with children being abused in the most horrendous way.[74]

Households that cannot meet their basic needs depend upon the income of their children for survival. Without the income from working children, parents in poor households may have to choose which child to feed. Moreover, schooling is expensive in most of the developing countries. Thus proactive measures of enforcing child labour laws by national governments, supported by provisions for social and economic security to the families with support from international organizations, business houses and national government is likely to go a long way in protecting and eliminating child labour even if globalization process exists (Globalization and Child Labour Linkages in India, Bupinder Zutshi, 2002).

REFERENCES

1. M. Prasada Rao. 2006. *Child Labour: Problems and Policy Issues*. Ambala: The Associated Publishers. pp. 1-4.
2. L.B. Punecha. 2006. *Child Labour: A Social Evil*. New Delhi: Alfa Publications. pp. 2-5, 33.
3. Kailash Satyarthi and Bubider Zutshi. 2006. *Globalisation, Development and Child Rights*. New Delhi: Shipra Publications. pp. 8-12, 29, 30.
4. Janet Hilowitz, Joost Kooijmans, Peter Matz, Peter Dorman, Michaelle de Kock, and Muriel Alectus. 2004. *Child Labour: A Textbook for University Students*. Geneva: International Labour Office. p. 16.
5. Joseph Gathia. 1998. *Approaches to Combating Child Labour in India. Caritas India Quarterly*: Vol. 48 (4). p. 12.
6. P. Anandharajakumar. 2004. *Female Child Labour.* New Delhi: A P H Publishing Corporation. pp. 4-5.
7. Daman Ahuja and Mahavir Jain. May 1998. *Economics of Child Labour-A Myth*. Kurukhshetra: Vol. 46 (8). p. 4.
8. UNESCO, *International standard classification of education (ISCED)*, Paris, 1997, which states that the customary or legal age of entrance to primary schooling, is not younger than five years.
9. *System of National Accounts 1993* (Brussels/Luxemburg, New York, Paris, Washington, D.C., Inter-secretariat Working Group on National Accounts: Eurostat, IMF, OECD, United Nations, and World Bank).
10. ILO. 1982. *Resolution concerning statistics of the economically active population, employment, unemployment and underemployment*, Thirteenth International Conference of Labour Statisticians (Geneva, ILO, October 1982).
11. For further explication of the concept "economic activity", see R. Hussmann, F. Mehran, V. Verma. 1990. *Surveys of economically active population, employment, unemployment and underemployment: An ILO manual on concepts and methods* (Geneva, ILO, 1990).
12. See ILO/IPEC (2004).
13. Note that child labour figured prominently on the agenda of the 18th

International Conference of Labour Statisticians (ICLS), held at the end of 2008. The objective was to develop and adopt a set of global standards for child labour data collection and measurement, including agreed global statistical indicators on child labour and its worst forms.

14. Janet Hilowitz, Joost Kooijmans, Peter Matz, Peter Dorman, Michaelle de Kock, and Muriel Alectus. *Op. Cit.* pp. 40-41.
15. *Ibid.* p. 41.
16. H. Cunningham. 1991. *The Children of the Poor*. Oxford: Blackwell.
17. Peter Doman. 2001. Child Labour In The Developed Economies. Geneva: ILO-IPEC. p. 40.
18. Child Labour Series. Dec. 1993. *Working Children in India.* Child Labour Cell: Noida. p. 7-8.
19. S.N. Mishra and Sweta Mishra. 2004. *Tiny Hands in Unorganized Sector-Towards Elimination of Child Labour.* New Delhi. Shipra Publications. p. 38.
20. *Ibid.* p. 39.
21. Mahavir Jain. 1994. *Child Labour in India-A Select Bibliography.* Noida: National Labour Institute. p. 4.
22. *Ibid.* p. 5.
23. Note that "child labour" is a narrower concept than that of "working children" or "economically active children". It includes all working children 5-11 years of age; excludes those in the 12-to 14-year age group engaged in "light work"; and, from among the 15-to 17-year-olds, includes only those in hazardous work or other WFCL. For more details see SIMPOC (2004).
24. Kailash Satyarthi and Bupinder Zutshi. 2006. *Globalization, Development and Child Rights.* New Delhi: Shipra Publications. pp. 71-72.
25. UNICEF. 2004. *The State of the World's Children 2004.* New York: UNICEF. p. 7.
26. See UNICEF. 1990. *First Call for Children: World Declaration and Plan of Action from the World Summit for Children.* New York: UNICEF.
27. *Ibid.* p. 6.
28. P. Anandharajakumar. *Op. Cit.* pp. 13-14.
29. "Children under the age of fourteen years may not be employed or work in any public or private agricultural undertaking, or in any branch thereof, save outside the hours fixed for school attendance, the employment shall not be such as to prejudice their attendance at school." Article 1 in: ILO. 1921. C 10: Minimum age (agriculture) convention. http://www.ilo.org/ilolex/cgi-lex/convde.pl.
30. June 26, 1973, 1015 U.N. T.S. 297, *entered into force June* 19, 1976 (Convention 138).

31. G.A. res. 44/25, annex, 44 U.N. GAOR Supp. (No. 49) at 167, U.N. Doc. A/44/49 (1989), entered into force Sept. 2, 1990.
32. UNICEF. 2000. *First Call for Children: World Declaration and Plan of Action from the World Summit for Children, Convention on the Rights of the Child.* New York: UNICEF.
33. 38 I.L.M. 1207 (1999), *entered into force* Nov. 19, 2000 (Convention 182).
34. Database of International Labour Standards. http://ww.ilo.org/ilolex/cgi-lex/ratifce.
35. D. Gibbons Elizabeth, Friedrich Huebler and Edilberto Loaiza. Nov. 2005. *Child Labour, Education and the Principle of Non-Discrimination.* New York: UNICEF Staff Working Papers Division of Policy and Planning Series. p. 1.
36. Confusion prevailed from the 1920s concerning the respective roles of the League of Nations and the UN in dealing with (child) slavery and of the ILO in dealing with child labour. This deficit regarding one of the worst forms of child labour persisted until 1999-2000.
37. C.K. Shukla, S. Ali. 2006. *Child Labour and the Law.* Sarup and Sons: New Delhi. p. 40.
38. Chanlett, Elisha Morier, G.M. 1968. *Declaration of the Rights of the Child.* Vol. XXII. International Child Welfare Review.
39. In 1976, the General Assembly proclaimed 1979 as the International Year of the Child. The general objectives were to promote the wellbeing of children, drawing attention to their special needs and encouraging national action, particularly for the least privileged and those at work. It was only during the IYC that international attention became fully re-focussed on the problem of child labour. The IYC acted as a spur to international agencies and civil society actors alike.
40. Alfred De Savza, (Ed.). *Children in India.* OXFAM India. p. 66.
41. UNICEF Publications circulated by UNICEF, Bhubaneswar India.
42. C.K. Shukla and S. Ali. b. *op. cit.* p. 41.
43. Alec Fyfe. 2007. *The Worldwide Movement Against Child Labour-Progress and Future Directions.* Geneva: International Labour Office. p. 8.
44. The idea of Wilfred Jenks was to consolidate the minimum age standards and to present a standard that developing countries would adopt.
45. Alec Fyfe. 2007. *Op. cit.* pp. 10-11.
46. Kofi, A. Annan. 2001. *We the Children.* New York: UNICEF. pp. 80-82.
47. C.K. Shukla and S. Ali. *Op. Cit.* b. pp. 41-42.
48. *Ibid.* p. 42.
49. ILO. 2008. *Quality Education is the Right Response to Child Labour.* ILO.

50. *Ibid.* p. 2.
51. Ramesh Kanbargi. 1991. *Child Labour in the India Subcontinent-Dimensions and Implications.* New Delhi: Sage Publications India Pvt. Ltd. p. 22.
52. Myron Weiner. 1990. *The Child and the State in India: Child Labour and Education Policy in Comparative Perspective.* Princeton: Princeton University Press.
53. Babita Agarwal. *Op. Cit.* p. 60.
54. http://www.savethechildren.org.uk
55. Gunther Martin and Caglar. 2003. *Child Labour in Europe and Central Asia.* Priliminary results of polls sponsored by UNICEF, with the Organization for Security and Cooperation in Europe (OSCE), Office for Democratic Institutions and Human Rights, April 2001.
56. International Programme for the Elimination of Child Labour. 2003. *Combating Child Labour Through Education.* Geneva: ILO.
57. Babita Agarwal. *Op. Cit.* p. 69.
58. http://www.un.org/womenwatch/conference/.
59. Janet Hilowitz, Joost Kooijmans, Peter Matz, Peter Dorman, Michaelle de Kock and Muriel Alectus. *Op. Cit.* p. 153.
60. *Ibid.*
61. World of Work. Dec. 1996. *Targeting the Intolerable.* Geneva: ILO. p. 7.
62. P. Anandarajakumar. *Op. Cit.* pp. 57-58.
63. Neeti Mohanti, April 1997. Gender Perspective in Child Labour. *Social Welfare*: Vol. 44 (1). pp. 10-11.
64. P. Anandarajakumar. *Op. cit.* p. 61.
65. UNICEF. 1990. *Children and Development in the 1990's.* New York: A UNICEF Source Book.
66. Edmons, Eric V. 2003. *Child Labour in South Asia.* France: Directorate for Employment, Labour and Social Affairs. pp. 28-29.
67. Alessandro Cigno, Furio C. Rosati and Lorenao Guorcello. 2002. *Does Globalization Increase Child Labour.* IZA DP No. 470.
68. Kallash Satyarthi and Bupinder Zutshi. *Op. Cit.* p. 208.
69. Eric Edmonds and Nina Pavcnik. 2006. "International trade and child labour: Cross-country evidence." *Journal of International Economics* 68: 115-140.
70. Edmonds, Eric and Nina Pavcnik, 2005. *The effect of trade liberalization on child labour. Journal of International Economics.* 65: 401-419.
71. Kailash Satyarthi and Bupinder Zutshi. *Op. Cit.* p. 210.
72. *Ibid.*
73. *Ibid.* p. 211.
74. *Ibid.* p. 215.

2

CHILD LABOUR IN INDIA

India is the world's third largest economy in terms of purchasing power parity (PPP), with a gross domestic product (GDP) of US $4.042 trillion. It is the twelth largest economy in the world when measured in exchange-rate terms, with a GDP of US $930.0 billion (2007). It is the second fastest growing major economy in the world, with a GDP growth rate of 9.2 per cent at the end of the second quarter of 2006–2007. However, due to its huge population, it has a per capita income of $3400 at PPP and $714 at nominal. The World Bank has placed it in the list of low-income economy. India's economy is diverse, depending on agriculture, handicrafts, textile, manufacturing, and a multitude of services.

The two-thirds of the Indian workforce depend directly or indirectly on agriculture. However, the service sector also plays an important role in India's economy. India's major industries include textiles, chemicals, food processing, steel, transportation equipment, cement, mining, petroleum, machinery and software.

India is a major exporter of highly-skilled workers in software, and financial services. Due to continuous economic expansion, India has made significant progress in reducing its federal fiscal deficit. However, the massive growth of population is the fundamental social, economic, and environmental problem.

Millions of children in today's world undergo the worst forms of child labour which includes Child Slavery, Child prostitution, Child Trafficking, Child Soldiers. In modern era of material and technological advancement, children in almost every country are being callously exploited.

United Nations estimate that there were 20 million bonded child labourers worldwide. Based on reliable estimates, at least 700,000 persons to 2 million, especially girls and children, are trafficked each year across international borders. Research suggests that the age of the children involved is decreasing. Most are poor children between the ages of 13 and 18, although there is evidence that very young children even babies, are also caught up in this horrific trade. They come from all parts of the world. Some one million children enter the sex trade, exploited by people or circumstances. At any one time, more than 300,000 children under 18-girls and boys-are fighting as soldiers with government armed forces and armed opposition groups in more than 30 countries worldwide. ILO estimates that domestic work is the largest employment category of girls under age 16 in the world.

India has the dubious distinction of being the nation with the largest number of child labourers in the world. In India, the government itself in its most recent account estimates that 12.6 million children under the age of 14 are at work in various occupations including hazardous occupations. NGO estimates put the number of children employed in domestic work and roadside eateries alone at two million. Centre of Concern for Child Labour, a Delhi based NGO estimated that there are nearly 70 million school-age going children in India who are out of schools. So the total number of working children in India is much higher than the government estimates.

The child labourers endure miserable and difficult lives. They earn little and struggle to make enough to feed themselves and their families. They do not go to school; more than half of them are unable to learn the barest skills of literacy. Poverty is one of the main reasons behind this phenomenon. The unrelenting poverty forces the parents to push their young children in all forms of hazardous occupations. Child labour is a source of income for poor families. They provide help in household enterprises or of household chores in order to free adult household members for economic activity elsewhere. In some cases, the study found that a child's income accounted for between 34 and 37 per cent of the total household income. In India the emergence of child labour is also because of unsustainable systems of landholding in agricultural areas and caste system in the rural areas. Bonded labour refers to the phenomenon of children working in conditions of servitude in order to pay their debts. The debt that binds them to their employer is incurred not by the children themselves but by their parent. The creditors cum employers offer these loans to destitute parents in an effort to secure the labour of these children. The arrangements between the parents and contracting agents are usually informal and unwritten. The number of years required to pay off such a loan is indeterminate. The lower castes such as dalits and tribal make them vulnerable groups for exploitation.

The environmental degradation and lack of employment avenues in the rural areas also cause people to migrate to big cities. On arrival in overcrowded cities the disintegration of family units takes place through alcoholism, unemployment or disillusionment of better life etc. This in turn leads to emergence of street children and child workers who are forced by their circumstances to work from the early age. The girls are forced to work as sex-workers or beggars. A large number of girls end up working as domestic workers on low wages and unhealthy living conditions.

Sometimes children are abandoned by their parents or sold to factory owners. The last two decades have seen tremendous growth of export based industries and mass production factories utilizing low technologies. They try to maintain competitive positions through low wages and low labour standards. The child labourers exactly suit their requirements. They use all means to lure the parents into giving their children on pretext of providing education and good life. In India majority of children work in industries, such as cracker making, diamond polishing, glass, brass-ware, carpet weaving, bangle making, lock making and mica cutting to name a few. 15 per cent of the 100,000 children work in the carpet industry of Uttar Pradesh. 70-80 per cent of the 8,000 to 50,000 children work in the glass industry in Ferozabad. In the unorganized sector child labour is paid by piece-by-piece rates that result in even longer hours for very low pay.

Inadequate schools, lack of schools, or even the expense of schooling leaves some children with little else to do but work. The attitudes of parents also contribute to child labour; some parents feel that children should work in order to develop skills useful in the job market, instead of taking advantage of a formal education. From the time of its independence, India has committed itself to be against child labour. Article 24 of the Indian constitution clearly states that "No child below the age of fourteen years shall be employed to work in any factory or mine or employed in any hazardous employment". The Bonded Labour System Act of 1976 fulfill the Indian Constitution's directive of ending forced labour. A Plethora of additional protective legislation has been put in place. There are distinct laws governing child labour in factories in commercial establishments, on plantations and in apprenticeships. There are laws governing the use of migrant labour and contract labour. A latest law The Child Labour (Prohibition and Regulation Act) of 1986 designates a child as a person who has not completed his 14th year of age. It purports to regulate the hours and the conditions of child workers and to prohibit child workers in certain enumerated hazardous industries. However there is neither blanket prohibition on the use of child labour, nor any universal minimum age set for child workers. All of the policies that the Indian government has in place are in accordance with the Constitution of India, and all support the eradication of Child Labour. The problem of child labour still remains even though all of these policies are existent. Enforcement is the key aspect that is lacking in the government's efforts.

Child workers are engaged primarily in agriculture and allied activities in rural areas and in a variety of industries and informal sector activities in the urban areas. The most exploitative form of child labour includes child prostitution and forced and bonded labour, which is found in some parts of the country. The situation of girl child labourers in the country would call for particular attention. Children today often labour under extremely hazardous conditions, handling poisonous chemicals, inhaling noxious fumes, hauling excessive weights. They are usually overworked, underfed and underpaid—if they are paid at all. They toil so that their families can survive. The painful voices of working children can be heard the world over and India is no exception.

With growing export, new areas of employing child labour are emerging. Garment units, embroidery units are now increasingly in news for violating child labour laws. In Rajasthan, the stone quarries employ under-age workers. Further north, in the state of Uttar Pradesh, hand-knotted carpets are made and sent to showrooms in America informs NGO Rugmark. Child labour is rampant here.

Child labour has emerged as an increasingly important issue in the national context reflecting heightened sensitivity to the problem at all levels within the country. The December 1996 Supreme Court judgment directs the withdrawal of children from hazardous occupation and the creation of a welfare fund for them, besides regulating working conditions in non hazardous occupations. Government policy has also been pro active in the area of child labour since the mid 1980 with the formulation of national policy on Child Labour in August 1987 and subsequent implementation of National Child Labour Projects.

Child labour is banned in 13 industrial sectors and 52 types of work listed in the Child Labour (Prohibition) Act. These sectors will not be able to employ children between 14 and 18 years if the law is amended. A 2006 amendment brought domestic work; work in the hospitality industry, under the ambit of the Act. But NGOs have been saying that despite the under-14 ban, thousands of children are still employed in hazardous industries listed in the Act, only due to poor implementation of the existing legislation. Save the Children's research on child domestic labour shows that 74 per cent of children in domestic work are between the ages of 12 and 16. This leaves a crucial gap in bringing a huge number of working children (aged between 14 and 18) under the protection of this Act.

Thousands of children work in roadside food stalls. Although India banned children under 14 from working as domestic servants or in food stalls, millions are continue to be employed, a study said. About 200,000 children below the age of 14 years are estimated to be working as domestic servants and in teashops, restaurants, spas, hotels, resorts and other recreational centres-the areas from where they were banned in 2006. Current child legislation is not effective. 'Save the Children' said that in Delhi alone, close to a million children are still employed at homes or in food stalls. Another 40,000 work in the southern city of Hyderabad and 50,000 more work in Calcutta. The study said that in Delhi 99 per cent of child domestic workers are girls and in a large number of cases they are open to sexual abuse.

Many parents say crippling poverty forces them to send their children, sometimes as young as five or six, to work in other people's homes or in factories. The Constitution of India and successive governments have targeted elimination of child labour and promoted universalisation of education. This task is not easy and the effectiveness of child labour elimination programme must be measured by real change in the situation of children and or by the number of projects funded and networks created or by the research, advocacy educational campaigns or workshops and seminars held or legislations introduced. As Kailash Satyarthi, chairperson of the Global March Against Child Labour, has put it, "The real measure of success is the difference being made in the lives of vulnerable children."

It is important to acknowledge here that since the adoption of the 1989 CRC and particularly the 1999 ILO Convention (No 182) concerning the 'prohibition and immediate elimination of the worst forms of child labour' a commitment to the abolition of child labour as human rights imperative has taken hold and begun to spread. The problem of child labour continues to pose a challenge before the nation. Government has been taking various pro-active measures to tackle this problem. However, considering the magnitude and extent of the problem and that it is essentially a socio-economic problem inextricably linked to poverty and illiteracy, it requires concerted efforts from all sections of the society to make a dent in the problem. Way back in 1979, Government formed the first committee called Gurupadswamy Committee to study the issue of child labour and to suggest measures to tackle it. The Committee examined the problem in detail and made some far-reaching recommendations. It observed that as long as poverty continued, it would be difficult to totally eliminate child labour and hence, any attempt to abolish it through legal recourse would not be a practical proposition. The Committee felt that in the circumstances, the only alternative left was to ban child labour in hazardous areas and to regulate and ameliorate the conditions of work in other areas. It recommended that a multiple policy approach was required in dealing with the problems of working children.

Government has accordingly been taking proactive steps to tackle this problem through strict enforcement of legislative provisions along with simultaneous rehabilitative measures. State Governments, which are the appropriate implementing authorities, have been conducting regular inspections and raids to detect cases of violations. Since poverty is the root cause of this problem, and enforcement alone cannot help solve it, Government has been laying a lot of emphasis on the rehabilitation of these children and on improving the economic conditions of their families.

Nature of Child Labour in India

Child labourers are divided into four main sectors including cultivators, agricultural labourers, manufacturing in household industries and others which includes construction workers etc. Most of the child labourers are involved in unorganized sector where they loose their childhood. A majority of the working children are concentrated in the rural areas. About 60 per cent of them are below the age of 10 years. Business and trade absorb 23 per cent while work in households' covers 36 per cent. The number of children in urban areas who work in canteens and restaurants, or those engaged in picking rags and hawking goods, is vast but unrecorded. Among the most unfortunate ones are those employed in hazardous industries. For instance, the fireworks and match box in Sivaski in Ramanathanpuram district in Tamil Nadu employ 45000 children. The lock making industry of Aligarh in Uttar Pradesh employees between 7000 and 10000 children below the age of fourteen years, accounting for 9 to 11 per cent of all workers. In the glass industry of Firozabad in Uttar Pradesh, 50000 children are working with a total workforce of 2 lakh workers.

In a study on the impact of development on the rural women in western Uttar Pradesh, as many as 83 out of 245 girls in 6-11 age group (about 33.5 %) were found to be engaged in some economic activity. Over 52 per cent of the girls in the age group 11-18 were similarly engaged. In Kashmir the carpet weaving industry employees small girls in back-breaking work. In another flourishing craft of this region-the fine hand embroidery-children are required to maintain the same posture for long hours and strain their eyes on intricate designs. This often leads to permanent physical deformities and eye damage.

The surveys of the metropolitan and mega make shocking revelations. Mumbai has the largest number of child labourers. In Varanasi, 5000 children work in the silk weaving industry. Even in Delhi, 60000 children work in dhabas, tea-stalls and restaurants. In the mining sector, 56 per cent of workers are children below 15. In most cases, children are favoured as they are docile and hence can be exploited.

Causes of Child Labour

In a country like India where over 30 per cent of the population is living in conditions of extreme poverty, child labour is a complex issue. Children work out of necessity and without their earnings (however meager they may be), the standard of living of their families would decline further. A large number of them do not even have families or cannot count on them for support. In these circumstances, the alternative to work may be idleness, destitution, or worse, crime.

Employers give certain justifications for employing children to suppress their guilt feelings. They say that the work keep children away from starvation. They are prevented from committing crimes which they would have indulged in if they had no jobs. The bureaucrats hold that the total eradication of child labour is not feasible because the government cannot provide substantial alternative employment to them. The social scientists say that the main cause of child labour is poverty. The children either supplement their parents' income or are the only wage earners in the family. It is said that 29.9 per cent of the total population of India or about 25 crore 23 lakh people live below poverty line. Of these, 20.6 crores are living in rural areas and 5.17 crore in urban areas. The highest number of persons living below the poverty line are found in Uttar Pradesh (4.48 crore), followed by Bihar (3.36 crore), Madhya Pradesh (2.24 crore), and Maharashtra (2.14 crore) (Rajasthan Patrika, November 13, 1994). These persons are forced to send their children to work in factories, etc. Another reason is that child labour is deliberately created by vested interests to get cheap labour. The third reason forwarded for the existence of child labour is that it benefits industries.

Bonded Child Labour in India

The most inhuman and onerous form of child exploitation is the age old practice of bonded labour in India. In this, the child is sold to the loaner like a commodity for a certain period of time. His/her labour is treated like security or collateral security and cunning richmen procure them for small sums at exorbitant interest rates.

The children are sold as bonded labour only to get a handful of coarse grain to keep them alive in return for their labour. Sometimes their period of thrall extends for a lifetime, and they have to simply toil hard and depend on the mercy of their owners, without any hope of release or redemption. The impoverished parents of the bonded child is usually a poor, uneducated landless labourer and the mortgagee is traditionally some big landlord, money lender or a big business man who thrives on their vulnerability to such exploitation. The practice of bonded child labour is prevalent in many parts of rural India, but is very conspicuously in the Vellore district of Tamil Nadu. Here the bonded child is allowed to reside with his parents, if he presents himself for work at 8 a.m. every day. The practice of child bonded labour persists like a scourge to humanity inspite of many laws against it. These laws although stringent and providing for imprisonment and imposition of huge fines on those who are found guilty are literally non-functional in terms of implementation.

However most of their efforts were sabotaged by high level government officials covering the fact that children were doing bonded work in factory premises. They deliberately employed their energy in running public awareness campaigns and made claims of creating propaganda against child labour, instead of punishing erring employers and freeing and rehabilitating the bonded children.

Neff also identified a major link between caste and bondage in Indian society. Dalit family's functions as bonded labour due to caste based discrimination and violence and not poverty in many cases. The caste system in India is one of the main foundations on which the edifice of bonded labour rests. Dalits or the so called untouchable are denied access to land in India, forced to work in inhuman conditions, and expected to perform labour for free. This is due to the so called upper castes boycotting them socially and subjecting them to economic exploitation. This attitude of society keeps the poor families bonded in a scourge of perpetual poverty and labour. It is now very important for all international donors to put pressure on the Indian government to enforce bonded labour and child labour laws in the country.

In India bonded labour has been illegal since 1976 when

parliament enacted the Bonded Labour System (Abolition) Act. However, the practice is still widespread. Even conservative estimates suggest that there are at least 10 million adult bonded labourers in India. 89 per cent of adults in debt bondage belong to schedule castes and tribes and 89 per cent of those who control them are agricultural landlords. Most of the work carried out by bonded labourers is hard manual labour in the fields or brick kilns. Children or adults are bonded in order to pay off debts that they or members of their families have incurred. They toil all their lives and endure physical attacks that often amount to torture.

There are thousands of bonded child labourers in India. They are also mostly the children of parents who belong to schedule castes and tribes. Young children are sold to employers by their parents to pay back small loans that they have borrowed. Such children are made to work for many hours a day over several years. According to one study, there are about 10 million bonded child labourers working as house servants in Indian families. Gursharan Varandani recently estimated that there were nearly 55 million children in India working as bonded labourers in agriculture, mining, brick-kilns, construction work, fishing activities, carpet weaving, fireworks, matches, glass moulding, bidi-making (cigarettes), gem-cutting and polishing work, electroplating, dyeing, washing and domestic work. About 20 per cent of these bonded child labourers were sold to cover some small debts obtained by their parents, usually for some social celebration like a wedding in the family.

Causes of Bonded Child Labour

Slavery in India dates back at least 1,500 years. Various forms of debt bondage co-existed with formal slavery. Poverty and tradition is one of the main reasons behind bonded child labour in India. No doubt, nimble fingers argument and other myths with illiteracy and ignorance of the masses is responsible for the existence of the institution in the present day modern and globalized world. A number of myths underlie and perpetuate child labour, justifying it on the grounds that the system "benefits" everyone involved: the country, the community, the family, the craft and the child.

The nimble fingers theory is applied to some of the harshest industries employing children, including the carpet, silk, beedi and silver industries. Agriculture employs far more bonded labourers, child and adult, than all industries and services together. It accounts for about 64 per cent of the general working population, 85 per cent of the bonded working population overall, and 52 to 87 per cent of the population of bonded child labourers. Conditions for bonded agricultural labourers are among the harshest to be found, work days are extremely long, payment is nominal and may consist of entirely of two meals a day and a yearly set of clothing, and the work is grueling.

Agricultural bondage is the oldest form of slavery known in India: accounts of agricultural bondage date back some 1,500 years. Of all forms of bondage, agriculture is most closely linked to caste; the caste system is most deeply entrenched in rural areas. Landlords are high caste, small landowners are of lower caste, and the landless and bonded labourers are primarily the Dalits (the oppressed). In rural areas, the master-slave relationship between the castes is not confined to land but permeates every aspect of village life.

Child labour is inextricably linked to bonded labour. In Andhra Pradesh, 21 per cent of the bonded labourers are under sixteen. In Karnataka, 10.3 per cent and in Tamil Nadu 8.7 per cent belong to this age group. A study shows that at the time of entering bondage, many labourers are as young as five years old. In Orrissa, common way of clearing debt is to sell daughters, eight to ten years old, as maid servants to the creditor. In several parts of the country, bonded fathers, over 40 years old, free themselves by deputing their sons into bondage. In the tea garden of Assam where employment of children below 12 years is prohibited, girls who bring food to their working mothers are encouraged to stay back and help with the work. Children mostly boys, have an important role to play in mining operations. While men do the digging inside the pits, boys carry coal to the surface. Children below 12 are preferred because their height allows them to walk without bending in the tunnels. Preference for child workers is most common in the unorganized sector because here it is relatively easy for employers to circumvent laws.

Magnitude of Child Labour in India

Since ages, the prevalence of child labour phenomenon is common in India. India has the largest number of world's working children. According to the Ministry of Labour and other NGO's estimate, there are 55 million children in labour force at present other than those working directly for their parents. Out of those there are 25 million children employed in agricultural sector, 20 million in service jobs (hotels, shops, and as servants in homes) and 5 million in the handloom, carpet making, gem cutting and match making industries. Ninety one per cent of child labour in India is in rural areas while nine per cent is in urban areas. In rural areas children have always helped around the farm and in production of its various rich handicrafts. In the present complex social set-up, characterized by the use of energy and technology for mass production of different kinds of products, handicraft sector is still of immense importance in India and men, women and children are busy with the said sector.

Table 2.1: State-wise Distribution of Working Children according to 1991 and 2001 Census in Age Group 5-15 Years

State/Union Territory	*Census 1971**	*Census 1981**	*Census 1991**	*Census 2001*
Andhra Pradesh	1627492	1951312	16,61,940	13,63,339
Assam	239349	.	3,27,598	3,51,416
Bihar	1059359	1101764	9,42,245	11,17,500
Chhattisgarh	—	—	—	3,64,572
Gujarat	518061	616913	5,23,585	4,85,530
Haryana	137826	194189	1,09,691	2,53,491
J&K	70489	258437	—	1,75,630
Karnataka	808719	1131530	9,76,247	8,22,615
Madhya Pradesh	1112319	1698597	13,52,563	10,65,259
Maharashtra	988357	1557756	10,68,418	7,64,075
Manipur	16380	20217	16,493	28,836
Jharkhand	—	—	—	4,07,200
Uttaranchal	—	—	—	70,183
Orissa	492477	702293	4,52,39	3,77,594
Punjab	232774	216939	1,42,868	1,77,268
Rajasthan	587389	819605	7,74,199	12,62,570
Tamil Nadu	713305	975055	5,78,889	4,18,801
Uttar Pradesh	1326726	1434675	14,10,086	19,27,997
West Bengal	511443	605263	7,11,691	8,57,087
Delhi	17120	25717	27,351	41,899
Goa	—	—	4,656	4,138

Source: The Indian Child: A Profile, 2002, Department of Women and Child Development, Ministry of HRD, Govt. of India.

* Census figures 1971, 1981 and 1991.

But in case of life conditions of children in the handicraft sector, they are suffering physically, economically, mentally and in all other areas of social life. Children can be seen performing a number of jobs in the handicraft sector, which by their very nature, are hazardous to their physical and mental growth and development. The net effect of participation of children in work is generally negative and harmful to their proper physical, mental and moral growth. In India every third child is working child and every fourth child in the age group five to fifteen is employed.

The increase in population has given rise to a considerable extent in the number of young persons in most of the countries, especially in third world. It is disheartening to note that thirty six per cent of Indian population is below fifteen years of age. In many developing countries the proportion of children below fifteen years has been between forty and fifty per cent of the total population. The increase in the proportion of children in recent years has significantly swelled the number of children working at low wages in different types of employments, particularly in the unorganized sectors.

In India working children are engaged in different organized and unorganized sectors. In rural areas children are engaged in fields, plantations, domestic jobs, forestry, fishing and cottage industry. In urban areas they are employed at houses, shops, restaurants, small and large industries, transport, communication, etc. In India working children are also self employed as newspaper boys, milk boys, shoe-shine boys, rag pickers, rickshaw pullers, potters, etc. As per 1971 census, while ninety two per cent of child labour in rural areas is engaged in primary sector, viz. cultivators, livestock, fishing and plantation, agriculture labour, etc. According to the 1981 census, 78.71 per cent of child workers are engaged in cultivation and agriculture, 6.3 per cent are employed in fishing, hunting and plantation, 8.63 per cent in manufacturing process, repairs, house hold industry, etc. 3.21 per cent in construction, transport, storage, communication and trade and 3.15 per cent in other services.

There are considerable variations between the states with respect to child labour. Work participation rates are high of children in the states of Jammu and Kashmir (10.53 per cent), Karnataka (7.92 per cent), Madhya Pradesh (7.9 per cent), and Meghalaya (7.92 per cent). According to 1971 census work participation rate of children were highest in Andhra Pradesh (9.24 per cent), in Kerela the percentage of child workers is only 1.08 per cent which is lowest among the states.

The distribution of child labour in different states appears to indicate certain co-relations. States with a larger population living below the poverty line have a higher incidence of child labour. A higher incidence of child labour is accomplished by a high drop-out rate in schools. The incidence of child labour is partly linked to the level of socio-economic development of an area and partly to the attitude of the parents, employers, and socio-cultural compulsions. The state-wise distribution of child labour in eleven major states in percentage terms, according to 1991 census is as fallows.

The Government of India has been taking several initiatives to reduce the problem. After passing the Child Labour (Prohibition and Regulation) Act 1986, and formulating the National Child Labour Policy 1987, the Government started National Child Labour Projects (NCLP) and set up the National Authority for the Elimination of Child Labour (NAECL) in 1994. In 1992, the International Labour Organization (ILO) launched the global programme, International Programme on the Elimination of Child Labour (IPEC) to work progressively towards elimination of child labour. India was the first country to sign a MOU with ILO in 1992, and altogether one hundred action programmes to cover 0.95 million children have been taken up under IPEC from 1992 to 2002. Till March 2002, Child Labour Projects have been sanctioned for rehabilitation of nearly 2.11 million children in hundred districts in the country. The package of services under NCLP includes special schools to provide non-formal education, vocational training, supplementary nutrition, stipend, health care, etc. Concrete efforts towards elimination of the child labour are being planned to be taken up in the eleventh plan to eliminate child labour in a convergent and time bound manner.

According to ILO, India contributes to about a 3rd of Asia's Child Labour and a 4th of world's working children. India has the largest number of working children in the World (between 60 to 115 million). In 1997 UNICEF estimated "child labourers in India as 73 million of whom 15 million are said to be bonded and stated that the condition of 70.6 million in the age group of 5-14 years who had not gone to school was not known. Child labour has been a way of life in India. In the earlier days grazing and looking after cattle and other domestic animals were always considered as the work of the rural children's especially boys. Urbanization and increasing poverty of the rural population compelled many rural families to migrate to cities. Children belonging to these families started taking up work as assistants in shops and establishment, hotels and restaurants and small scale workshops. Exploitation of the children is not a new phenomenon. It existed in India even prior to independence. Subsequently an effort was made to prevent abuses of child labour by legislation. But it remained mostly un-implemented.

Families need money to survive, and children are a source of additional income. Poverty itself has underlying determinants, one such determinant being caste. When analyzing the caste composition of child labourers Nangia (1987, p. 116) observes that, "if these figures are compared with the caste structure of the country, it would be realized that a comparatively higher proportion of scheduled caste children work at a younger age for their own and their families' economic support". Scheduled caste children tend to be pushed into child labour because of their family's poverty. Nangia (1987, p. 174) goes on to state that in his study 63.74 per cent of child labourers said that poverty was the reason they worked.

The combination of poverty and the lack of a social security network form the basis of the even harsher type of child labour—bonded child labour. For the poor, there are few sources of bank loans, governmental loans or other credit sources, and even if there are sources available, few Indians living in poverty qualify. Here enters the local moneylender; for an average of two thousand rupees, parents exchange their child's labour to local moneylenders (Human Rights Watch 1996, 17). Since the earnings of bonded child labourers are less than the interest on the loans, these bonded children are forced to work, while interest on their loans accumulates. A bonded child can only be released after his/her parents make a lump sum payment, which is extremely difficult for the poor (Human Rights Watch 1996, 17). Even if bonded child labourers are released, "the same conditions of poverty that caused the initial debt can cause people to slip back into bondage" (International Labour Organization 1993, 12).

Even though poverty is cited as the major cause of child labour, it is not the only determinant. Inadequate schools, lack of schools, or even the expense of schooling leaves some children with little else to do but work. The attitudes of parents also contribute to child labour; some parents feel that children should work in order to develop skills useful in the job market, instead of taking advantage of a formal education.

The Census 2001 Reports

Population Aged 5-14 years

- The total population of the persons, aged 5-14 years in the country is 2531.64 lakhs. Out of this, 1323.68 lakhs (52.29 per cent) are males and 1207.96 lakhs (47.71 per cent) are females.
  - Out of the total population, aged 5-14 years, 126.67 lakhs (5.00 per cent) are workers and 2404.97 lakhs (95.00 per cent) are non-workers.
  - Amongst the total work force, 57.80 lakhs (45.62 per cent) are main workers and 68.87 lakhs (54.38 per cent) are marginal workers.
- The share of workers aged 5-14 years in the total workforce of the country works out to be 3.15 per cent.

Table 2.2: Distribution of State/UTs as Per Share of Workers Aged 5-14 Years in the Respective Population Total

Range (%)	*State/UT*
0-2	Goa, Delhi, Pondicherry, Kerala and Lakshadweep.
2-4	Tamil Nadu, Maharashtra, Uttarakhand, Punjab, Tripura, Andaman and Nicobar Is., Daman and Diu and Chandigarh.
4-6	Manipur, Jharkhand, Assam, Haryana, Bihar, West Bengal, Orissa, Gujarat and Uttar Pradesh.
6-8	Andhra Pradesh, Chhattisgarh, Karnataka, Madhya Pradesh, Jammu and Kashmir, and Arunachal Pradesh.
8-10	Dadra and Nagar Haveli, Nagaland, Rajasthan, Meghalaya and Himachal Pradesh.
10 and above	Mizoram and Sikkim

Source: International Labour Office (India). 2007. Child Labour Facts and Figures: An Analysis of Census 2001. Geneva: ILO.

- The State/UT with the highest share of workers aged 5-14 years in the total workforce of the State/UT was Sikkim (6.26 per cent).
- The State/UT with the lowest share of workers aged 5-14 years in the total work force of the State/UT was Lakshadweep (0.18).

Table 2.3: The Distribution of Total Workforce Aged 5-14 Years as Per Census 2001 in Different Industry Categories at All India Level

Industry Category		*Percentage*
A (Agriculture, Hunting and Forestry) and B (Fishing)		20.28
C (Mining and Quarrying)		1.06
D (Manufacturing and Repairs)	NHI	22.53
	NHHI	25.48
E (Electricity, Gas and Water supply)		0.11
F (Construction)		5.75
G (Wholesale and Retail Trade)		10.02
H (Hotels and Restaurants)		1.71
I (Transport, Storage and Communications)		1.77
J (Financial intermediation) and K (Real Estate, Renting etc.)		1.26
L (Public Administration etc.) to Q (Extra Terrestrial Organizations and Bodies)		10.03
All Categories		100.00

Source: International Labour Office (India). 2007. Child Labour Facts and Figures: An Analysis of Census 2001. Geneva: ILO.

- As compared to 1991 Census, there has been an increase of 10.68 per cent in workers aged 5-14 years in 2001 Census (excluding the State of Jammu and Kashmir).
- Between 2001 and 1991 in terms of absolute number, the category of Main Workers aged 5-14 years has decreased considerably by well over one-third (36.97 per cent).
- However, over the same period there has been a manifold increase of Marginal Workers aged 5-14 years (207.10 per cent).

A similar comparison of workers aged 5-14 years across different State/UTs (Jharkhand, Uttrakhand and Chhattisgarh has been merged to Bihar, Uttar Pradesh and Madhya Pradesh respectively for comparison) reveals table 2.4.

Child Labour and Kashmir

The frontier state of Jammu and Kashmir, though endowed with rich grandeur natural beauty and resources, have been one of the most economically backward states of the country. Due to various socio-economic, political and geographical factors, agriculture, which is the main stay of nearly eighty per cent of the population, has remained under developed due to many inhibitions. The most important natural

Table 2.4: Workers Aged 5-14 Years Across Different States/UTs showing percentage decline in 2001 as compared to 1991 State/UTs witnessing percentage increase in 2001 as compared to 1991

State/UTs Showing Percentage Decline in 2001 as Compared to 1991	*State/UTs Witnessing Percentage Increase in 2001 as Compared to 1991*
Dadra and Nagar Haveli (-3.22), Gujarat (-7.27), Goa (-11.13), Karnataka (-15.74), Orissa (-16.53), Andhra Pradesh (-17.97), Lakshad-weep (-20.59), Daman and Diu (-22.53), Kerala (-24.84), Tamil Nadu (-27.65), Maharashtra (-28.49), and Pondicherry (-28.96)	Madhya Pradesh 95.71), Assam (7.27), West Bengal (20.43), Punjab (24.08), Tripura (32.03), Uttar Pradesh (41.71), Arunachal Pradesh 949.11), Delhi (53.19), Andaman and Nicobar Is. (54.94), Meghalaya (55.75), Mizoram (60.05), Bihar (61.82), Rajasthan (63.08), Manipur (74.84), Himachal Pradesh (90.96), Chandigarh (102.09), Haryana (131.10), Nagaland (178.43) and Sikkim (193.98)

Source: International Labour Office (India). 2007. *Child Labour Facts and Figures: An Analysis of Census 2001.* Geneva: ILO.

resources of land, water, forests, minerals, etc, existing in the state have remained unexplored and untapped.

The state is particularly deficient in the field of industrialization. However, after independence, particularly since the introduction of economic planning in 1953 the state has been able to register unprecedented socio-economic development. But inspite of this the state is economically backward, twenty five per cent of population was found living below poverty line in 1993-94, though the below poverty line population has decreased now to a considerable extent. The number of poor persons has remained almost the same between 1973-74 and 1993-94. According to NSSO 1997, 2.2 million children enrolled of a child population of 3.1 million, 35 per cent drop out at middle level entry, under weight children 44.5 per cent and 41 per cent with stunted growth. Violence since 1989 in Jammu And Kashmir State has brought unprecedented sufferings to people. The conflict has disturbed the social fabric, damaged the economy, disturbed the source of livelihood of thousands of families and in many cases deprived the family of its breadwinner. Children and women of the Kashmiri society have gone through a gruelling trauma over recent times because of the armed conflict situation. The most disturbing fallout of it has been the nominal increase in destitution manifest in the rise in the number of orphans, widows, the invalid and the disabled.[1]

The population of the state, according to 2001 census, is 10169,763, which is a little under one per cent of the country's total population. The total working population is around thirty five per cent of the total population of the state, but just less than one per cent of the working population of the country. Statistics on the extent of employment of children are available to a limited extent. The majority of the child labour is engaged either in agriculture or form related work or in the unorganized sector. This sector accounts for children working as domestic servants, carpet weavers, embroidery, chain stitch, wood carving, leather, embroidery, paper machi, willow works, zari embroidery, gaba making, pottery, wayside, shops, and shoe-shine boys, etc. According to the 1981 census, the incidence (main/marginal workers) of total child labour force in the state of Jammu and Kashmir was 10.53 per cent of the total working force. Child labour is more prominent in district Baramullah fallowed by Anantnag where number of children working in different sectors of economy account for 23043 in 1981 which constitutes 18.34 per cent of the total child labour force working in Kashmir division. Out of this number 12305 were males and 10738 were females. The 1991 census put the number of children in District Baramullah (27703) followed by district Anantnag. District Budgam occupied the third place and Kupwara was happiest in the sense that child labour force constitutes only (10.06 per cent) of the total child labour force in Kashmir division.

The statistics shows that institution of female child labour is not very much common in Kashmir division. The reason for less female child labour appears to be social rather than any other. Due to social factors keeping females at home, parents not like to send their female children to work outside their homes.

The Census 2001 Reports

The total population of the state is 101.44 lakhs. Out of this, 53.61 lakhs (52.85 per cent) are males and 47.83 lakhs (47.15 per cent are females. Out of the total population, 37.54 lakhs (37.01) per cent are workers and 63.90 lakhs (62.99 per cent) are non-workers. Amongst the total workforce, 26.09 lakhs (69.49 per cent) are main workers and 11.45 lakh (30.51 per cent) are marginal workers.

Table 2.5: District Wise Classification of Child Labourers (Main/ Marginal Workers) in Kashmir Division

Name of the District	*Year 1981*			*%*	*Year 1991**		
	Boys	*Girls*	*Total*		*Boys*	*Girls*	*Total*
1. Anantnag	12305	10738	23043	18.34	12613	11007	23620
2. Pulwama	9061	10755	19816	15.79	9288	11024	20312
3. Srinagar	12523	7286	19809	15.78	12836	7468	20304
4. Budgam	11312	11272	22584	17.97	11602	11554	23156
5. Baramullah	14144	12883	27027	21.52	14498	13205	27703
6. Kupwara	5755	7556	13311	10.60	5899	7745	13644
Total	65100	60490	125590	100	66736	62003	128739

Source: Census 1981.

* Computed and compiled by the scholar on two per cent advance tabulation of Census 1981 and it excludes Leh and Kargil.

Population Aged 5-14 Years

The total population of the persons, aged 5-14 years in the State is 26.53 lakhs. Out of this 13.67 lakhs (51.53 per cent) are males and 12.86 lakhs (48.47 per cent) are females. Out of the total population, aged 5-14 years, 1.76 lakhs (6.62 per cent) are workers and 24.77 lakhs (93.38 per cent) are non-workers. Amongst the total workforce, 0.55 lakhs (30.91 per cent) are main workers and 1.21 lakhs (69.09 per cent) are marginal workers. The share of workers, aged 5-14 years in the total workforce of the State works out to be 4.68 per cent.

Population Aged 5-17 Years

The total population of persons aged 5-17 years is 33.61 lakhs. Out of this 17.30 lakhs (51.48 per cent) are males and 16.31 lakhs (48.52 per cent) are females. Out of the total population, 26.38 lakhs (78.50 per cent) belonged to rural areas and 7.23 lakhs (21.50 per cent) to urban areas. Of the total population, 1.19 lakh (3.54 per cent) are main workers, 2.16 lakhs (6.42 per cent) marginal workers and the remaining 30.26 lakhs (90.04 per cent) are non-workers.

The share of workers aged 5-17 years in the total workforce of the state works out to be 8.92 per cent. Amongst the main workers, 0.80 lakh (67.43 per cent) are males and 0.39 lakh (32.57 per cent) are females. Of the main workers, 0.16 lakh (13.81 per cent) were attending educational institutions and 1.02 lakhs (86.19 per cent) were not attending any educational institutions. Amongst those who were attending educational institutions, 0.11 lakh (67.94 per cent) are males and 0.05 lakh (32.06 per cent) are females. Similarly, amongst those who were not attending any educational institution, 0.69 lakh (67.35 per cent) are males and 0.33 lakh (32.65 per cent) are females.

Statement of the Problem

The developmental needs of the children in the state have suffered as a result of variety of factors including the conflict situation for the last twenty one years. The education of children has been disturbed in a large number of cases. When child labour remains a serious issue of concern throughout the country, this issues gains an equally, if not more, significant attention in the state of Jammu and Kashmir especially because this issue has been largely neglected by the Government and the larger civil society. This is probably because of the priority that the government place in addressing the conflict issues.

Children instead of attending school and enjoying their childhood are engaged in earning a livelihood, often in harsh circumstances. Child labour is a complex socio-economic phenomenon, which is perpetuated by the poverty of families and the demand of the employers for cheap and docile labour. Children are almost entirely found employed in the unorganized sector. Child workers are exploited through low wages, arbitrary terms of employment, bad working conditions and long hours of work. They do not have the protective cover of the laws.[2]

Since the 1991 census was not conducted in Jammu and Kashmir, figures on the number of child workers are not available. In 1981, the number of child workers was reported by the census to be 109,000 main workers (those engaged in an economic activity for more than six months in a year) and 149,000 marginal workers (those engaged in an economic activity for less than six months in a year).[3]

The Supreme Court had directed in its judgment in December

1996 that a comprehensive survey be done to identify child workers. A survey done by the State Government in May 1997 reported 24,000 child workers in hazardous occupations in the Kashmir Division. The Government of India has requested that a re-survey be done in the state. The 2001 census shows the number of child labourers in Jammu and Kashmir as 1,75000 but the NGOs and other estimates show it more than two and a half lakh.[4]

The nature of work of child labour in Kashmir is similar to what has been found in rest of the country. In the absence of large scale industries children in the state mostly work in unorganized sectors like carpet industries, *papier-mâché*, wood carving, *crewel* work, willow work, embroidery, *zari* works, chain stitch, leather and fur works, transport workshops, repair houses, *namdas* and *gaba* making, domestic servants, hotels and restaurants, etc. It is also qualifying to note that the practice of bonded children has been done away with. Children of both sexes work in these fields/sectors in rural and urban areas and in organized and unorganized sectors. Generally, the life condition of these workers in terms of health, hygiene, diet, environment, education, economic standard, entertainment and so on are worse; several micro studies have revealed their life conditions as "horrible". As a result, a large number of these children develop acute and chronic diseases, which compels them to stop work. However, new children are readily available and are recruited in vacant places. These little workers work ten to fourteen hours a day, six days a week, but with least monetary benefits. In reality, there is no set standard for their wages.[5] They are paid according to wishes and whims of the proprietors, masters and other concerned. In the previous twenty two years of militancy in Jammu and Kashmir, these child labourers suffered more than other sections of society. However, the progress in Kashmir to meet the above can best be described as dismal since the priorities of the government and the administration has been continuously, for the past two decades, focused on maintaining law and order situation.

Contrary to the views and exhortations of philanthropists, social workers and thinkers for banning the child labour, the fact remains that there are some tinny sectors where a complete ban on child labour may not be desirable. Economic compulsion in these cases may not be the sole reason for child labour. It may be the survival of the very art or of the craft. This is more valid in Kashmir where certain delicate art crafts can best be performed by children alone. Many employers say, with pride that if we want to preserve our arts and crafts of Kashmir, then employment of children is necessary because of being done by the workers of tender age and soft wrists. They argue that child labour also exerts a downwards pressure on the wage rates for carpet-weaving which would otherwise become prohibitive. However, these arguments advanced by employers do not carry much weight. Child labour has given rise to a number of socio-economic problems. It is beyond doubt that children are forced by circumstances to do labour in tender age when they should have been in schools. The mere fact has been that it is not the work but labour that children are coerced to do which has manifold repercussions for them, for their families and for the society as a whole.[6]

REFERENCES

1. C.K. Shukla and S. Ali. 2006. *Child Labour-Socio-Economic Dimensions*. New Delhi. Sarup and Sons. pp. 1-15, 27-33.
2. Chandergupt S. Sanon. 1998. *Working Children: A Sociological Analysis.* New Delhi: APH Publishing Corporation. pp. 1-9.
3. C.K. Shukla, S. Ali. *Op. Cit.* a. pp. 1-2.
4. Department of Women and Child Development. 2002. *The Indian Child: A Profile.* Ministry of Human Resource Development: Govt. of India.
5. Nasir Ahmad Shah. 1992. *Child Labour in India.* New Delhi: Anmol Publications. pp. 1-29.
6. C.K. Shukla and S. Ali. 2006. *Op. Cit.* a. pp. 1-15, 27-33.

3
LITERATURE REVIEW

Child labour was in practice in Indian society from times immemorial. Children gave helping hands to their parents in the household chores and also in family occupations. Various Sanskrit books have described how children in Indian families shared the workload of their parents and of their gurus during their Brahmachary period (Study life). The famous story of Krishna and Sudama clearly establishes that children (students) were used by their gurus for carrying out certain household chores. In the modern period with the advent of new industrial culture this practice has assumed an alarming proportion only to attract the attention of social workers, philanthropists, and social activists to its various negative aspects. It was never a problem till children were used as helping hands. The need for more production at cheaper costs and the motive to earn more and more resulting in using the helping hands as working hands. Various social organizations and leaders took serious notice of this practice and made hue and cry. Consequently, it attracted attention of the government, parliamentarians and social scientists, which made several attempts to understand the problem from different angles. This chapter will make a modest attempt to review such efforts and link these findings with the present study on child labour in the handicraft sector.

Studies on Child Labour

Socio-demographic studies conducted so far provide some findings on the linkages between child work participation, schooling and poverty.

The Global Level Studies

The study by Mamadani in Punjab, India (1972) was probably the first to clearly articulate the view that peasants need high fertility for the economic benefits gained thereby. Mamadani also clearly made the connection between poverty and the economic gains of child labour, as well as those from grown up children. Mamadani's style is polemical and the anecdotal nature of the data seriously detracts from the work as empirical or scientific. On the other hand, it must be said that Mamadani's study made a forceful statement of the problem and showed the usefulness of an anthropological approach to data collection.

The study, however, meets few of the criteria listed in the previous section. Respondents are viewed as basing fertility decisions (i.e., respecting family planning) on economic considerations, but it is doubtful that the meaningfulness of fertility decision-making can be measured solely by attitudinal type responses. Contraceptive practice was generally low in the field study area, so in a sense the respondents lacked two clear alternatives about which they could make a decision.

An influential study of Cain in Bangladesh (1977) used data collected on the time-use of inhabitants from an agricultural village to support the conclusion that male children become net producers at an early age and more than cancel the costs they incur by 15 years. Activity is divided into 'enabling' labour and productive work, but the possibility of joint production is not contemplated. More importantly, the net result of the labour of children (such as baby-sitting and collecting fuel) in terms of adult members' activities thus enabled is not measured.

The problem of integrating the economic context into the study design is hinted at but never adequately taken into account. For example, Cain acknowledges that for the 23 per cent of households with no land, the chances of children finding wage employment were 'limited' and, at the same time, that most farming families hired labour at least occasionally. Hence, some kind of labour market must have existed in the study area which would compete with a household's supply of child labour. Cain infact alludes to this but does not systematically attempt to link hired labour with family supplied labour. Furthermore, as Lindert (1983) points out, the wage rates used in the study tend to exaggerate the value of child labour since peak-season rates were employed. Also missing in this study is any reference to schooling to how education may compete with child labour in the use of children's time. Altogether these calculations lead to an overly bright picture: children produce more than they consume by 13 to 14 years of age and become net assets by their early twenties. Furthermore, since there are no obvious externalities to cloud this picture (since villages are largely closed economic systems), over the years Bangladesh should have grown ever more prosperous.

The two related studies on Indonesia and Nepal (Nag et al., 1977) which use somewhat different data collection techniques have a similar objective of trying to determine the economic value of children by measuring child labour. The study reported economic activity and recorded that a distinction is made between 'directly productive' and 'household maintenance' work. In general, except that longer periods of field study eliminated the problem of peak-season bias. Furthermore, expressing child labour in terms of a proportion of an adult labour standard, as has been done in these studies, has the additional draw back of obscuring the possibility of adult unemployment. To the extent that adults are underemployed, child labour could be replaced without cost to the household as a whole if better uses of children's time arose. In view of the fact that few of the criteria listed are satisfied, little confidence can be placed in the tentative conclusion reached by the discussed studies, namely, that children have net positive economic value to their parents.

Although suffering from many defects, *the study by Vlassoff, 1978* differs in a number of respects. Much more attention was paid to the economic context of the study area and to the wide variety of arrangements by which labour was exchanged. The different interpretation which may be applied to the activity of children was also explored, although measuring productive work was probably not any more successful. Less reliance was placed on observing child labour and more on the value that fathers' perceived such labour to have. A main feature of the study was to link child labour (and old age security) with fertility and family planning behaviour, although the problem of casualty, it was acknowledged, prevented definite statements from being made based on the analysis of this relationship. More weight was given to attitudinal data precisely to circumvent the casualty problem, but the validity of such data is always somewhat doubtful, especially if the attitudinal questions are not subject to extensive prior testing. Finally, educational data were given prominence, mainly because it became apparent in the course of field work that education of children was a prime concern of parents despite the obvious increase in costs to parents that educating their children implied. Even though the main finding-that child labour probably does not motivate high fertility-is probably no more defensible than the opposite findings of the other studies reviewed, the chief merit of this Indian village study was to sound a warning by elucidating a number of conceptual and methodological pitfalls in this genre of empirical investigation.

Leah Levin (UNICEF) in their study in 1978 on child labour in Morocco's carpet industry observed that, "Morocco's laws prohibit the employment of children below 12 years of age and make a maximum working week for any age of 48 hours". The anti-slavery society team visited 62 factories of carpet weaving in Morocco. Except in 8 factories they found that all factories had employed little girls and in 28 of these factories about one-third of the workforce was found to be constituted by these girls of fewer than 12 years to fewer than 8 years of age. These children worked for more than 48 hours a week and some even more than sixty hours a week. Pay was found low for these children and even some of them did not get any emoluments.

The survey of children at work by Mendeleivich (UNICEF) in 1979, tried to highlight the problem of child labour in India and its causes. In fact, the problem of child labour in India may be seen as the result of traditional attitudes, urbanization, industrialization, migration, and lack of schools or the reluctance of parents to send their children to schools, etc. In the ultimate analysis main causes are extreme poverty and agriculture being the main occupation of the majority of population requiring more hands. Child labour is essentially a problem of the poor and destitute families, where parents cannot afford to provide education to their children. They treat children as additional hands who can supplement the family income which is inadequate. These people are struggling to get the minimum basic requirements of life and which most of the times took the childhood of the children in their families.

The study on Mexico conducted by Shuman, 1982, for which it was impossible to obtain more than an abstract, examines an *ejido* (communal village) in southern Mexico. This is the only relevant Latin American research that we know of. The study links fertility to the 'perceived relative value of children' and finds no significant relationship.

Of all the research reviewed here, only Lindert (1980, 1983) has taken cost data (other than presumed consumption of staple foods, as in Cain's investigation) into account as well as direct opportunity costs to parents. The overall finding is that in this setting, described as relatively 'affluent', children are never net assets. As noted by Lindert, the net cost of parents would be even higher if less conservative estimates of costs were used or if peak-season wages (the only ones available) were not used. It must be pointed out, however, that this study uses presumed average costs, these data not being collected for individuals. It is impossible to say, therefore, for a given family whether children were or were not net assets: this may be affected by the household type, the economic context of the family or by what adults do with the time 'supplied' to them by their offspring. Nor, as in the majority of studies reviewed, is any connection made to fertility.

This study on Tanzania by Kamuzora, 1984, is the study based on African data. Basically a time-allocation survey, the author uses as a starting point the idea that in Africa land is plentiful and abundant. Thus an economic context entirely distinct from the earlier Asian research is apparently being observed here. Perhaps because the original purpose of the survey was not related to child labour, the age groups used (5-9, 10-19, 20+) are not very illuminating. Even so, an odd finding is that boys aged 5-9 years contribute marginally more work than do youths aged 10-19 years. This leads to the thought that the definition of economic activity may have included activities that would have been classed as 'enabling' or 'household' tasks in other studies. Or, more probably, schooling may be subtracting from the labour input of the group aged 10-19 years.

Apart from presenting a breakdown of time allocation by these broad age groups, little else is contributed to the problem of child labour and fertility. What, superficially, appears to be evidence of excess supply of labour is countered by the not altogether convincing statement that 'in a peasant economy the demand for labour determines its supply'. Although no cost data were collected, the author suggests that the preference for school attendance over child labour in a context of poverty indicates that costs outweigh benefits.

National Level Studies

Srikantan et al. (1978) have studied child work participation in the integrated development of a command area. Their investigation shows that for the younger generation males aged five to nine years, the percentage were much higher for dependents than for earners in the three study groups used. This suggests that early work participation perhaps prevents (regular) attendance at school and leads to more illiteracy. Similar differences were observed for girls. Again, compared to the older generation, the younger generation had less literacy among earners and more literacy among dependents. This indicates the competition between work participation and schooling so that, among dependents, youths are more literate than adults of the same sex, whereas among earners, the contrary is true. The relationship between education and work participation of children is similar. These differentials tend to confirm the competing demands made on children by work participation and schooling, both on boys and girls, and especially among poorer families.

A study (Gopunjkar 1980) on the working children in the tribal areas of Maharashtra, conducted with a view to preparing a detailed note on different types of work children did, revealed that children participated in all the occupations/jobs available to them and activities of home/family occupations and kept themselves engaged throughout the year. The child starts working from about 5 to 6 years of age. The income from the work of the land is of two types in cash and in kind. Wages in cash are governed to some extent, by the Minimum Wages (amendment) Act of 1979. But in many cases labourers are paid less than what is due to them. The wages in kind are given at rates in accordance with the local practice. Except for a few activities like *Saldari*, children enjoy real free life and do not feel the constraints of work. They are not overburdened and feel free in the working atmosphere. However, proper education and health facilities are not available in the country. Diseases resulting from malnourishment and unhygienic conditions and practices are very common.

M. Singh, an Economist, in his study in Bombay (1980) found that 20.6 per cent of the interviewed employers were employing children because they were quick and efficient, 12.6 per cent preferred them because they were more amenable to discipline, some found them better suited for some types of jobs, 30.5 per cent said that their plight had greater sentimental appeal, 9.3 per cent were in favour of them as they were cheap and 1.9 per cent favoured because of their honesty. The majority (69.2 per cent) of the interviewed parents mentioned economic compulsions as the main factor. As many as (25.8 per cent) responded that the child was idle and doing nothing. Therefore, he/she was put to work to save him/her from the demoralizing effects of idleness. There were 69 (24 per cent) respondents who said that the child had left the school and there was no alternative but to put him/her at work and keep him/her busy. Sixty two of them (21.6 per cent) attributed the early entry to work on the part of their children to death, disease or loss of job of the earning member of the family. Some respondents said that their children were keeping bad company and slipping into delinquency so they had to put them on some job so that they might inculcate a sense of discipline. Still others mentioned that the child himself/herself was keen to earn; so they did not stop him/her from working. A few (10 per cent) said that the child was alone at home and, therefore, he/she was not safe to ensure his/her safety, they put him/her on some job.

Singh presents the working conditions of both self-employed and employed children. Self-employed child workers were found to be working for ten hours a day who earned an amount around hundred rupees per month on an average. The lack of fixed place of shelter, inadequacy of equipment and harassment by officials were the main problems in carrying out the job smoothly. According to their parents, work developed a sense of responsibility in their children, made them sober, considerable and well-behaved. The findings about the employed children revealed that none was asked to produce a certificate of medical fitness by the employer nor the employer got him/her medically examined. The children engaged in construction work, arts and crafts and production received the highest payments whereas those in households and restaurants were paid the lowest emoluments in terms of hard cash.

A survey by Gerry, an Economist in 1981, shows that carpet weaving is flourishing in the states of Tamilnadu, Uttar Pradesh and Kashmir. Employment of children in activities suited to them keeps the cost of production low. They also work as apprentices. In household carpet weaving enterprises children are considered indispensable as helpers and as trainees who continue the craft.

The study on problems and social services needs of child labourers in agriculture in Uttar Pradesh by Singh, an Economist in 1982, revealed that the average age of the child workers was 13.6 years while the majority of child workers (70.2 per cent) belonged to the age group of 13 to 18 years. The majority of the child workers were from non-tribal Hindus and Schedule Castes. The maximum number of child workers who discontinued the studies were in the age group of 8 to 12 years.

The causes which make the children to join the work force at a very young age according to a study on the *working children in Hissar by Sharma, a Sociologist, in 1982* were acute poverty of their family, death and chronic illness of the earning members and there was no source to supplement their family income. The social circumstances which also motivated the child workers to seek jobs were company of the friends, rude behaviour of parents and lack of affection in the family, etc.

Another report by Gangrade, an Economist, (1983), reveals that the states like Uttar Pradesh, Jammu and Kashmir and Tamilnadu have flourishing centres of carpet weaving. Varanasi, Bhodohi, Mirjapur are also big centres of carpet weaving. It is Mirjapur where fifty thousand workers are engaged in carpet weaving of which nearly twenty per cent are children.

One more study on the working conditions of children employed in unorganized sector, in Sivaski (CSR, 1984) found that children were the main bread winners in most of the families there. A large number of families depended on the income from match units either as main source or as supplementary source of family income. About 30 per cent of the families had more than two children employed in match units. Most of the children were under compulsion to work due to poverty. A majority (95 per cent) of them took up jobs in match units because of the poor financial conditions of their families. Another 6 per cent of them were interested to continue their studies but were forced by their parents to work to support their families or to supplement the family income.

While talking about child labour in Bhadohi region of Varanasi District in U.P., Ramesh Kanbargi, (1985), argues that, the main reason for the employment of children was that children had nimble fingers and keen eyesight and they could sit in the same posture for hours. Most of the children had low socio-economic family status. Children had no fixed hours of work and they work for 9 to 10 hours a day. Most of the workers worked even on holidays. The data on the educational achievement of the 49 children in the sample showed that only few children received 4 or more years of schooling. The study revealed that children working in the carpet weaving industry were regularly exposed to health hazards. Enquiry revealed that children suffered from many ailments such as fever, cough and colds, backache, diarrhoea and dysentery, skin infection, breathing problems, etc. Almost all the children reported that they liked their work.

One more study (Juyal 1985) conducted on child labour in Varanasi at the suggestion of a committee on Child Labour appointed by the Government of India, indicated that wages paid to the Child Workers varied from occupation to occupation. Similarly, the mode of payment of wages also varied from occupation to occupation. About 36.56 per cent employers said that they had child workers because they are cheaper, 27.13 per cent employed them due to easy availability. The hours of work and employers behaviour varied from occupation to occupation and depended on the nature of activities. However, in most of the activities, the working hours ranged from 9 to 15 hours. The environment of 198 work units was generally clear but dirty in 73 units. Out of 258 employers, as many as 206 (80 per cent) answered that they had not ever encountered any representative of the labour laws enforcement agencies coming to the unit for an inspection.

Kanbargi and Kulkarni (1986) have observed that age and gender constrain the quantum and nature of the gainful and domestic activities of children. While boys aged 5 to 7 years work, on the average, for about two hours a day, by 12 to 14 years they work for 5 hours a day. Boys put in more time tending livestock and working on the family farm or enterprise. Girls work for longer hours in very different activities from boys, such as in food preparation and domestic chores.

The daily time spent at school and in school-related activities does not increase appreciably with age for school-going children but the proportion of children at school declines sharply with age. This is reflected in the apparent decline, with age, of daily time spent on schooling among all children.

With an increase in the size of land owned or livestock held child work participation appears to increase, especially among labour-hiring families. The higher the father's level of education, the more likely are children to attend school. Scheduled caste families have the lowest school attendance rate for children whereas higher castes have higher rates. There are regional differences in child labour participation and the schooling of children.

In the state of Himachal Pradesh, a study on the problems of the working children revealed that about 1/3rd of the children of the age group of 10 to 14 years in rural and 1/8th of those in urban areas were at work in India. Children were working in agriculture and households, on an average work for 280 days in a year. In villages, children were used as bonded labour and as contract labour in urban areas. Of the working children, 36.79 per cent belonged to Schedule Castes and Scheduled Tribes, and 20.75 per cent to lower castes. Thus, incidence of child labour is much higher in economically backward communities. As regards their literacy, 71.52 per cent were illiterate.

Carpet industry in Rajastthan also exploits 'nimble fingers' of children to minimise costs and maximise profits. *Manju Gupta* observes that sometimes very young children of four to five years of age also work in the industry, in cottage units as well as in factories. Gupta's study shows that these children suffer from serious health risks, such as, strain, lung problem, malnutrition, stunted growth and general weakness. The worst part of these children is that they frequently work under constant fear of contractors, employers and even parents which affects their psychological development adversely. It is estimated by Gupta that a carpet that fetches Rs. 7041 in West Germany gives only Rs. 600 to two workers who work on it for 60 days.

Child Labour Studies in Kashmir

M.L. Pandit's study on Handicrafts in Jammu and Kashmir (1979) shows that handicrafts sector contributed 4.74 per cent of net state domestic product in 1978-79, and that the total production as well as the share have increased over the years. About 28 per cent of the work-force in this sector consists of child labour, of which 35 per cent belong to the five to nine year age group. The main crafts where children work are embroidery and carpet manufacturing where they work either as helpers (family units) or hired workers (non-household units). Pandit's study shows that about one-third of the children work for more than eight hours a day, about one-tenth of the children do not earn anything at all as they are 'learning', while the majority of them earn Rs. 2 to Rs. 2.50 per day. None earns more than Rs. 5 a day. These crafts are mainly for exports and the trade is in the hands of middlemen who make huge profits. Pandit observes that state legislations are inadequate and implemented indifferently.

A survey (Khatu, 1983) in Carpet viewing industry in Kashmir shows that about 80,000 to one lakh children between 6-14 years of age were engaged in carpet weaving. They work about 10-12 hours a day and earn a total of Rs. 10-15 daily.

Prof. Nisar Ali in 1987 while analyzing child labour in the carpet industry of Kashmir reveals that there were about 28.5 thousand working children in the handicraft sector. Out of the total child labour in the handicraft sector just a half percent exists in Jammu province. Almost the entire child labour was found in Kashmir. The study finds that 40 per cent children were illiterate and 70 percent working children were either illiterate or had education below primary level. Majority of children were in the age group of 10 to 14 years. The working hours were not according to some strict norms. Children were working for more than eight hours in majority of units. Majority of children get labour according to skill acquired. While explaining the causes of child labour, Prof. Nisar Ali argues that about 97 percent children attend carpet weaving due to poverty and the loan locations. The interior conditions were found to be hazardous except in some large scale industries/factories. Majority of carpet weaving children complained backache, abdomen pain and respiratory problem.

The findings of the study, *causes and consequences of child labour in Kashmir, by Nazir Ahmad Kutay and Miss Sabhia Malik in 2002,* revealed that the problem of child labour existing in Kashmiri society has wider ramifications. Taking into consideration the causes and consequences of the problem, the situation reflects an extremely cruel social situation which engulfs socially, economically and educationally backward communities. Mr. Kutay and Miss Sabhia found that the problem of child labour as existing in Kashmiri society has given rise to multidimensional problems having implications on one's physical, social, emotional, moral, and educational development. It is not only social apathy towards child labour but the government in this regard has also shown lack of interest; thereby the problem has become more complex and dangerous. Moreover, problem of social control, crime and social conflict emanate from the situation without proper care and response, on the part of government and society at large. The study was carried out in Srinagar district of the state, the findings revealed that male, female involvement in child labour was in the ratio of 70:30. The children aged below 14 years and involved in child labour in the unorganized sector were working as automobile workers, domestic savants, hawkers, cobblers, milkmen, shop helpers etc. Majority of the respondents were engaged in automobile workshops and as domestic servants to provide financial support to their poor families. Although a nice attempt on the part of the researcher but not without gaps. The study was carried out in Srinagar district only and based on a smaller sample which cannot represent the social characteristics of children under work in other parts of the state which are having different social settings and there is also a methodological concern of the study.

The research of Prof. B.A. Dabla, on the life conditions of child labourers in the handicraft sector in Kashmir, 2006-07, found that the main motivating agents for making the child labourers to join handicraft centres were parents, friends, relatives, self motivation, motivation by poverty conditions, etc. The study observed that majority of the child labourers had an experience of 3 to 6 years and the rest were in this business from last 7 to 10 years. It was found that four main areas of handicrafts work of *Shawl-Bafi, Kaleen-Bafi, Doen-Hutch Kaem*, and *Paper-Mache* are the dominant as well as common. Prof. B.A. Dabla observed that the basic and important facilities were not provided to the child labourers like, toilet-urinal, water, electricity, first-aid, heating arrangement, lunch, ventilation, etc. It was found that the child labourers are exploited to the maximum extent by employers as well as by parents of the child labourers through wages, work etc. The life long work of the child labourers in the handicraft centres has led to some disastrous, chronic diseases and life long disability among the child labourers, like weak eye sight, mental stress etc. Majority of the child labourers interviewed were drop-outs from schools. The study observed that while majority of child labourers (over 90 per cent) and parents (over 80 per cent) favoured the abolition of child labour, the least number of employers (below 25 per cent) favoured the abolition of child labour. It is because the employers earn the maximum possible profit through child labourers. Although a fine piece of work by Prof. B.A. Dabla, but he missed in interpreting many important aspects of child labourers which should have been otherwise touched by the study. Another important critic of the study is that it was based on a smaller sample and the findings of which cannot be generalized. The study also touched only a specific sector where child labourers are working and ignored other sectors.

The study undertaken among *Child Labourers in the Handicraft Sector in traditional and transitional Purki community in district Kargil of Kashmir (2008), by Bilal Ahmad* in order to ascertain the phenomenon of child labour in its proper perspective. Under the present study, distribution of families by religion of the working children shows that 58.46 per cent were Muslims and 41.53 per cent were Buddhists. Infact Bilal has written a competent thesis on the question of child labour in the handicrafts home industry in Kargil. It is centred on the pathology of an institution, around which many laws have been passed. Bilal has successfully discussed the findings where he has debated the issues involved in child labour based on a well designed methodology. However, the truth is, his thesis communicates that the poverty of people forces them to continue to send young children to work.

A wider range of aspects such as family, economic status, parental perception, education, gender discrimination, middle men dimension and exploitation, relations of production, cultural acceptance, and issues of health and recreation, etc. have been covered, but what is missing in the thesis is the sense of village and town, the relationship between rural and urban networks, for surely production is related to the hinterland of rural production, as well as the urban nexus of markets, including international ones, or tourist communities. Mr. Bhat has concentrated on existing rules, and the breaking of these rules. Within that framework, he has given valuable data on family structure, poverty and its indexes including level of education, occupation and health, as parameters of understanding the life of these children. The health conditions are particularly bad and require careful reading so that we may understand the life chances of these children who work on carpets, *papier mache* and other objects which are an integral part of the tourist trade. Infact, Bilal has done a careful statistical analysis of many different aspects of child labourers in Kargil, but there is a need of further focus on more qualitative indexes which will give a sense of the relations between town and country, between tourism and political environments, between commerce and consumption and human rights.

Book Review

The work of *Sharad D. Gokhale and Neera K. Sohoni*, 1979, *Child in India,*[1] reviews the situation of children from the standpoint of demography, policy, legislation, programme intervention, evaluation, research, and training and resource requirements. The author points out that India is an ancient country growing young. According to 1971 census, 42 per cent of Indian population comprises of below 14 years of children. In discussing children in India and their quality, it is worthwhile considering the surroundings they are in, the health standards in which they are maintained, the educational equipment they are provided with, and the activity in which they are engaged. The health standards of children are bound to be low in a country where 40 per cent of the rural and 50 per cent of the urban population lives below subsistence. The author narrates that child labour in India is a multidimensional problem. Various demographic, social and economic forces work in unison to determine the magnitude of the child labour force. Important among them are high fertility, resulting in a young population structure and abundant availability of children for work, high economic value for children as the society is mainly traditional and agricultural activities which do not require skill or training, low levels of schooling and a larger number of school dropouts. The enormous size of the child population certainly puts pressure on child education. No country in the world has a separate plan for children. Yet, in accordance with UN's children charter, all nations are honour bound to protect and promote fundamental rights of children. Planning for children, or planning even for the community as a whole, is a technical function; it is and should be the exclusive responsibility of specialized agencies, knowledgeable and skilled in the planning tasks at various levels. The phenomenon of planning would also include parents, teachers, health personal, nutritionists, social workers, administrators, home science and extension workers, etc. to plan for children, in sum, is to achieve a break through in the evaluation of the next higher stage in 'socio-biology', mentions the author.

The study by *S.K. Tripathy*,[2] *Child Labour in India*, 1989, studies the problem of child labour in Indian society in depth keeping in view the causes, nature, dimension, magnitude and most importantly its social implications. It notices the importance of children as the future citizens of our society and rightly tries to make us aware to protect and preserve both physically and mentally our future (crop). The author explains child labour as employment of children in gainful occupations or a material contribution to the income of the family. Child labour is both an economic as well as a social problem. In developing countries like India children are employed in almost every sector like agriculture, domestic services, street trading, shops and commercial establishments, construction and manufacturing units, handicraft sector, etc.; inspite of the hazards involved in those occupations for these little children. Child labour persists in inverse relation to the degree of economic advancement of a society, country, or region. It has got different effects on different societies. The extent of it in rural areas has influence on rural emigration and again the participation of young workers reduces the work opportunity for adults. According to the author every third household in India has a working child and every fourth child in the age group of 5 to 15 is employed. The child workers in our country are working in unsatisfactory conditions in unorganized sectors for long hours with low wages in ill-ventilated, ill-lighted and dirty work places. They are badly treated by their employers who misuse their energy and skill paying them very low amounts in return. The author points out that child labour is economically unsound, psychologically disastrous and physically as well as morally dangerous and harmful. It deprives him/her of education, training and skills which are the necessary prerequisites of earning power and economic development. The labour legislations are ineffective. Many laws, legislations, amendments and other constitutional measures were passed from time to time but all get failed.

The work entitled, *Child Labour in India*,[3] 1990, is a study of socio-economic perspectives of child labour in India by *Amarnath Singh,* an Economist. Child as we know is said to be the father of man and a citizen of tomorrow. In India family enjoys little recognition without child. Historically, it is found that the practice of child labour is very old in India. The increase of population and higher poverty rates forced parents to send their children to undertake some job and is common in India both in organized and unorganized sectors in all the states and union territories. The present volume by Amarnath Singh studies a study conducted in the unorganized sectors by the Centre for Social Research, Madras in 1984 revealed that about 54 per cent of child labourers had been working for more than two years. They worked for longer hours, i.e., more than 10 hours per day even in ill-ventilated places without basic amenities and rest which affect their health and retard their physical and mental growth and development in early age. The reason for employment of children varies from culture to culture or from group to group in the same culture or society. Children are trained in their family occupations. The traditional system of employing them in family occupations and economic necessities are the major causes of child labour points out Amaranth Singh.

The study, *Child Labbour in The Indian Sub-Continent-Dimensions and Implications,*[4] 1991, by Ramesh Kanbargi, an eminent Sociologist, highlights that though the ultimate goal of governments in less developed countries is to totally eradicate child labour, the existing socio-economic and cultural factors, along with the conceptual, definitional and measurement problems associated with child labour pose a serious hindrance in achieving these goals in a reasonable time. The author points out that today child labour is almost non-existent in the industrialized countries where it was prevalent during earlier times. However, the predominance of child labour in many third world countries continues to be quite pronounced. By and large, the greater the importance of agriculture and related activities, the greater is the use of child labour. Besides agriculture, cottage industries, handicrafts and other similar activities are not generally covered by a minimum age at entry or other protective legislations. The continued existence of child labour in many third world countries is also partly due to the inadequate educational opportunities in these countries. The developed countries can afford greater investment in education for their children and can keep them in school for more years. In addition in countries where most people live at subsistence or below subsistence levels, children are often forced to work to supplement family income. The author concludes that children work because people have children, rather than people have children because children work. The author quotes Cetris Paribus, the less the number of competing obligations (such as school) and the greater the opportunity, the more time will be spent performing such household tasks. But many other factors are likely to be involved, including cultural dispositions. It is premature to conclude that child labour motivates high fertility in less developed countries and even less justified to claim that poor rural families need child labour to survive.

The volume Indira Hirway, Jacqui Cottyn and Pushkar Pandya, 1991, *'Towards Eradication of Child Labour: An International View'*[5] is based on collection of papers presented in an international seminar on child labour in New Delhi by scholars from diverse fields. Jacque Cottyn discusses in the volume about the world peace and defined it in the context of 'Democratic Socialist Declaration of the Rights of Children'. Inequitable distribution of land, poor access of the weaker sections to resources, gradual destruction of the environment, existing socio-political systems-all put so many constraints on the poor that they are forced to use the meagre incomes of children to support themselves. Whether it is the child labour in the handicraft sector in Kashmir, child workers in the lock industry in Aligarh, child labour in the carpet industry in Rajasthan, child labour in trade unions, jari industry, etc., the authors have presented it in a very lucid and composite form given by different researchers and scholars. Not only this, the scholars and researchers provide useful suggestions and recommendations for the solution of the problem.

The present volume also discusses child labour in many developed countries and brings out the fact that child labour exists in developed countries also but its magnitude and dimension is very less in these nations because they have controlled the issues and causes giving birth to such problems. No doubt child labour is prevalent in well off nations but the conditions under which they work are less damaging and hazardous to the health and physique of the young children. If the institution of child labour is prevalent there, it is because of some poverty and educational system related issues, etc. In nut shell the authors discuss that it is comparatively nonexistent in developed nations. Amongst the important suggestions the paper presenter's presented, the authors ultimately reached to the conclusion that politically, there is a need of strong government that is not subservient to foreign interests in the country and is truly for the benefit of the majority of the people. And culturally, we have to learn new technology for self management and self determination. This needs educational campaigns that will create awareness and bring about people's participation.

The work entitled '*Child Labour in India*' by Nazir Ahmad Shah,[6] 1992, discusses the employment of children in different sectors of the economy as a faitaccompli of any and every Human Society, be it underdeveloped, developing or the developed one. The author points out that the onslaught of industrial and technological revolutions coupled with the changing life styles have added new dimensions to the whole problem. As a matter of fact the problem is vexed and widespread. The adverse impact of child labour can be seen in the form of educational backwardness, economic exploitation, moral deterioration, health hazards and in many other forms highlights the author. Article 24 of the Indian constitution says that 'no child below the age of fourteen shall be employed to work in any factory or mine or employed in any hazardous employment. The numerous Acts like the Child Marriage Restraint Act of 1929 (Sarda Act), The Employment of Children Act 1938, The Factories Act, 1948, The Plantation Labour Act, 1951, The Mines Act, 1952, The Children (Pledging of Labour) Act, 1935, etc. have been passed from time to time to safeguard the interests of the children under work discusses the author.

About the working children in Kashmir the author comes to the conclusion that children working in the handicraft sector, etc. suffer from a variety of problems both physical and psychological. Besides it mars their growing personality and plunges the nation into gloom and darkness. Our future generation is thus abused, exploited, and assaulted. The author at the end provide suggestions for the solution of the menace amongst which protective legislation, welfare programmes (health care facilities, grant of stipends, playing facilities, etc.), education facilities, voluntary organizations for child welfare, need for seminars and workshops, registration of units, fixation of working hours and minimum wages, provision of good working conditions, public awareness, attack against poverty, etc. are included on priority basis. This volume on child labour by Nazir Ahmad, infact throws light on almost all aspects of the child labour but what I found missing is town and country relationship, globalization, human rights and child labour, commerce and trade and economic and political environment.

The Indian Child Labour,[7] 1994, by, *Jinesh C. Kulshreshtha* gives the utmost importance to child and clarifies that it is beyond the state of doubt that politically, socially and economically child is the seed of nation's future. Conscious of this indisputable fact, the constitution of India is enshrined with the directive principles and also contains specific provisions under fundamental rights-for according protection to children against exploitation by unscrupulous agents, and for ensuring his/her physical, intellectual and moral development but unfortunately they fall much short of. Almost the entire unorganized sector still remains untouched by child labour legislations and executive orders. This happens to be the unfortunate state when our country has the largest quantum of child labour. J.C. Kulshrestha uses the term child labour in two different ways, first, as an economic practice and secondly, as a social evil. It is in the second context that the term child labour is now more generally used. Child labour therefore assumes the character of social problem in as much as it hinders and arrests or distorts the natural growth processes and prevents the child from attaining his full bloom manhood. It would be good to remember that child labour not only affects the children themselves but it ultimately affects the whole of the society and the nation. The author has also projected the extent and the working conditions of the child labourers in various economic sectors in India including factories, industries, agriculture and in other organized and unorganized sectors which is pathetic and miserable and get worst day by day and the role played by the trade unions, political parties, voluntary organizations and the mass media in improving the working conditions of children and for better enforcement of the child labour laws.

Varandani Gursharan's, 1994, *'Child Labour and Women Workers'*[8], discusses the two basic components of the labour force whose exploitation by the employers has become a matter of disgrace and humility particularly in third world countries. The child labour is a social evil and has late attracted the attention of global organizations including ILO, UNICEF, etc. as it poses a serious challenge to most of the developing countries including India. The author has discussed child labour and women workers-a complex issue on various grounds which include low wages, long working hours, bad working conditions, etc. in comparison to the adult and male counterparts.

The book discusses the role of International Labour Organization for combating child labour, by having different conventions for this purpose from time to time. As India is having the largest number of child labourers in the world, their present working conditions, wage and other aspects have been discussed in detail. The author reviews both the literature on child labour, as well as the laws and commissions which have drawn attention to this malpractice. Plight of child labour working in match industry, bidi making units, carpet and glass industry, lock industry, in pottery, tea gardens, as domestic labourers, etc. has been dealt with full concentration and analysis. The author points out that the state has failed to discharge its duty in the right earnest so far as the child labour is concerned.

The book discusses The Child Labour (Prohibition and Regulation) Act, 1986 in detail and tries to highlight its loopholes. It has also brought into notice the legal protection extended to child workers under other labour legislations in India and discussed legal protection to women labour in the light of myth and reality. The current trends and position of employed women in different countries has been also discussed in the light of international perspectives. Lastly the author provides some useful suggestions in prohibiting employment of children in various sectors of economy where they are working.

Child Labour in Unorganized Sector,[9] by *Mittal Mukta*, 1994, is one which is a comprehensive, short and lucid but an informative and empirical volume on the pathology of an institution, around which many laws have been passed and framed. The author discusses the issue existed in different forms from the dawn of civilization whether in agriculture, crafts and trades or in any other sector. In the world of poor people, the practice of child labour is more prevalent no doubt but the evil in one or the other form is present in the developed world too though with less intensity. In the countries of Africa and Asia due to its cheapness and unorganised form, it is preferred. The study by Mittal is based on a programme having field investigations of the art of *chicken* embroidery in Lucknow, the capital of UP in India, performed by children of under age. The study shows that *chicken* embroidery art is presently performed by Muslim female child labourers only as it is having a history behind it. Family tradition makes them to take up this work. All the indexes including personal profile, family, educational and health determinants of child labourers has been discussed in detail. Other aspects like working conditions, economic determinant, living environment and recreational determinant of child workers are dealt with enough seriousness and attention.

No doubt the present volume of Mittal on the pathology of an institution has been compiled on the research study empirical in character and having a well built research design and methodology, but what I found missing is the sense of village and town, the relationship between rural and urban networks, for surely production is related to the hinterland of rural production, as well as the urban nexus of markets, including international ones or tourist communities.

Kulshrestha C. Jinesh, 1996, *Child Labour in Indian Lock Industry*,[10] discusses the importance of child as the future crop of the mankind. The rights of the child against violence and exploitation in home, work place, etc. through UN conventions and at the country level through legislations, etc. are discussed with care and concern. The author has also discussed in elasticity the magnitude of the problem. Poverty, low wages of the adult, unemployment, migration, big families, traditional attitudes, illiteracy and ignorance, etc. have been explained in length as the factors responsible for the emergence of child labour.

The next chapter of the study deals with the measures to protect the child from the damages of the labour in tender age. The author has discussed the issue in different countries of the world including England wherein the Government in 1536, enacted a legislation which empowered the justices of peace and other officials to bound beggars and spoilt children between the age of five to fourteen years to agriculture or crafts. The book also discusses elaborately the child labour history in America, Russia and India. The author has also highlighted the legislative measures enacted in connection with the institution of child labour taken from time to time not only in India but in many developed countries of the world.

Infact the present volume by Kulshrestha is based on a study entitled 'Child Labour in the Lock Industry of Aligarh' UP India. No doubt the locks prepared by lock industry in Aligarh are famous in the country, but the conditions under which children work, the process of lock making, working hours, nature of work, wages, etc. are dangerous not only to their physical, social and moral development but also destructive for their future social and individual life. The author discloses the fact that how violation of the protective laws is taking place in the lock industry of Aligarh.

The author, at the last discusses the need for a national consensus for protecting the colourful flowers of our beautiful garden, the society. The problem is a multidimensional one, and it, therefore, needs a multidimensional solution also. The suggestions recommended by the author for the solution of the phenomenon of child labour stretch from legislative measures to constitutional provisions. At the implementation level the author suggests the effective enforcement of the child labour laws and the active cooperation of the public, social workers and non-governmental organizations. Last but not the least, the campaign for creating awareness in the public mind against the evil of child labour must be intensified through educational programmes and wide publicity.

G.P. Mishra, P.N. Pande, 1996, in *Child Labour in Carpet Industry,*[11] studies how child labour deprives the child of his or her inalienable natural rights to education and normal healthy growth. But the irony of the fact is that child labour persists as an integral part of the labour process of production on a large scale in the country, discusses the author in the introductory part of the present study. This phenomenon darkens the human face of development when the twentieth century is heralded with scientific and technological surfeit. Why children in millions work for paid or unpaid wages in hazardous industries or occupations, despite having child labour prohibitive legislative measures, is not only socio-economic issue but also a question relating to natural justice and human rights.

In the present book an attempt has been made to study the question of child labour in the context of hand-made carpet industry belonging to Mirzapur in Uttar Pradesh. The present study shows (a) why the households supply child labour for wages in the labour market; (b) how the child labour is used and abused; and (c) the implications of child labour use and abuse on the physical development and health of the working children in the industry. So far as the health conditions and social infrastructure are concerned, they are bad and resulted in the physical underdevelopment of the working children. The lack of medical and health facilities has resulted into many health problems. The perception and attitude of working children about their work is also discussed in this study. To what extent the labour laws and other Government measures have been effective in curbing the use and abuse of child labour is discussed too. In the end the author has discussed critically the legal status and other aspects of child labour including the Child Labour (Prohibition and Regulation) Act, 1986, so that to open the loopholes of the various laws for curbing child labour institution. An overall finding of the study shows that child labour is being reproduced due to the given socio-economic situation and the specific nature or form of production in the concerned industry.

The authors have studied the socio-economic background of sample households and the supply of child labour in detail. Pattern and distribution of household income, indebtness and consumption pattern, child population and supply of child labour, etc. have also been studied under the socio-economic background heading. Mishra and Pande have also dealt with socio-economic conditions of working children and their labour use through different indexes which they have treated statistically and analysed sociologically. Pattern of wage income and child labour use, etc. is also analysed sociologically.

Airyn de Tenorio, 1998, *Child Labour in Domestic Service,*[12] an instructional manual based on a 1998 IUF/ILO seminar held in Nairobi, Kenya on how trade unions can combat child labour in domestic service. Manual is divided into six sections:

1. Addresses general issue of child labour and demographics of child labour in Africa.

2. Focuses on working, living, and socio-economic conditions of child labourers in domestic service sector.
3. Reviews national and international legal framework, including ILO, national, and international legislation.
4. Reviews national and international policy-making strategies and how trade unions can use legal mechanisms in efforts to eliminate child labour.
5. Addresses policy development within trade unions and areas where trade unions can concentrate efforts.
6. Presents action plans and strategies based on current trade union action, work of NGOs, Kenyan Ministry of Labour, and other sources.

Manual concludes with a guide to planning a one-day child labour seminar, which includes a model training agenda, facilitator notes, and handouts, slideshows, and groups activity ideas. Model programme is designed to be adapted for use by unions in other industries and countries.

Francesco D'Adamo's "Iqbal"[13], 1998, is a sensitively written young-adult novel that gently brings readers into the brutal reality of child slavery in modern-day Pakistan. The novel is based on the life of Iqbal Masih, a Pakistani child crusader and activist, sold, like many poor children, into virtual slavery-working the handlooms in a carpet factory to pay off their parents' debts. Iqbal was an exceptionally bright and fearless boy-eventually he escaped to become a leading light in the crusade to end this cruel practice. He was awarded the Reebok Human Rights Award, traveled internationally, and spoke out passionately against the system that kept children shackled to lives of indefinite labour. Sadly, he was murdered in 1995 at age 12 under murky circumstances in his village.

D'Adamo's spare, evocative novel is told through the eyes of a young girl, Fatima, who labours next to Iqbal, weaving rugs. It's an interesting choice and makes for a curiously muted but deft book. Through Fatima, we come to see what an extraordinary and vital presence Iqbal was. The minute he arrives in the dim, cramped factory, the story throbs with tension. No one knows what Iqbal will do, and the suspense as his defiance grows-including slashing a fine rug-makes for a compelling story.

The book is strongest when depicting the claustrophobic world of these children, as they survive and are subtly transformed by Iqbal and his quest for freedom. D'Adamo gives us a bleak and moving sense of their lives: their blistered and bleeding fingers, the high window in the factory that delivers only a sliver of light, and the horrific "Tomb," an underground cistern where the children are sent for punishment. One of the most moving moments is when the children have finally escaped to a house run by activists, and Fatima wakes up the first morning disoriented and in a panic: "My first thought was: I'd better get to the loom. It's late and the master will punish me."

Because the story is told through Fatima, parts of Iqbal's life are rendered off-stage and are less satisfying. His transformation from a boy who burns with injustice to an articulate leader who interacts with the wider world is slightly lost. And the public Iqbal, who by all accounts became an extraordinary speaker, helping to lead the international campaign against the sale of rugs made by children, never fully comes to life.

Marita Ishwaran (edited by Caroline D'Souza and Jaya Menon), 1999, *Violation of the Child's Human Rights: "Street Children," "Child Labour," and "The Girl Child",*[14] Bombay, Research and Documentation Centre, Justice and Peace Commission, Asian Human Rights School, published three modules on children's rights excerpted from a larger Justice and Peace Commission human rights curriculum and adopted by the Asian Human Rights Commission as part of their on-line human rights correspondence course. Each module is designed to fit a thirty five-minute class period, and content and case studies are focused exclusively on Asian countries, especially India. Chapter I, "Street Children," introduces the UNICEF definition of street children, categories of street children, and provides several short case studies and testimonials from children. Chapter II, "Child Labour," defines child labour according to Indian law, suggests major causes of child labour, and reviews national (Indian) and international efforts to eliminate child labour. Chapter III, "The Girl Child," introduces the concept of gender discrimination and gives examples of how girls in India experience concrete forms of oppression, including premature and exploitative forms of work, and ends with discussion questions to accompany the video "Let Her Die" and a script of a role play for participants to perform. Each module ends with suggestions for group activities, suggestions to coordinate lessons with national holidays recognizing children's rights, and ideas on how participants can connect directly with child labourers to offer support, carry out interviews, and develop action campaigns.

'Children's Life worlds: Gender, Welfare and Labour in the Developing World'[15], *by Olga Niewenhuys*, 1999, examines how working children face the challenge of having to combine work with school. Moving beyond the usual concern with child labour and welfare to a critical assessment of the daily work routine of children, this book shows how class and kinship, gender and household organization, state ideology and education influence and conceal the lives of children in developing countries. Presenting an extraordinary sympathetic and detailed case study of the daily work routines of the boys and girls in a village in southern India, the book shows how children negotiate the value of their work. The combination of personal experience, quantitative data and in-depth anthropological analysis sheds light on the world of peasant children, a world that social anthropology has largely neglected.

Working from a conscious commitment to bridging the gap in knowledge between the world of childhood and that of adulthood, *Children's Life worlds* discusses how working children face the challenge of combining the demands of the school with the need to contribute to the household income. At a time when many developing countries are extending children's education, the author focuses on the way children balance the demands made on them by the adult world, how they view childhood within that world, and how, ultimately, children too make history. The first chapter of this book presents one of the best critical analyses of the literature examining children's work to date. Child labour is viewed as a social construction and the author gives a central place to the process through which work is undertaken and acquires its meaning. This book reveals the author's life-long commitment to understanding the gamut of issues relating to working children, especially among the rural poor of Kerala. That subjectivity makes this work a rare gem and does "elicit solidarity rather than pity" for children's life worlds.

Robert McIntosh, an employee at the National Archives of Canada, has written an interesting book on *'Boys in the Pits: Child Labour in Coal Mines'*[16], Canada in the 19th-and early 20th-centuries.

Boys in the Pits, 2000, explore the history of boys, aged 8 to 15, who worked in the coal mines in Canada. They laboured underground, leading horses along lengthy and treacherous subterranean roads, manipulating ventilation doors, helping miners cut and lift tons of coal, and filling wagon after wagon with freshly-mined coal, as the first step in its removal from the mines. For young boys, the work was very hard, as justified by their role in producing the energy that fueled Canada's Industrial Revolution.

The author examines how the various roles of changing technology, alternative sources of unskilled labour, and legislation concerning the children from 1820 to 1940—which eventually banned children in the mine and required compulsory education—affected Canadian society, as it moved from the Industrial Age into the modern era. One British author of a child labour book argues that, "the exploitation of little children, on this scale and with this intensity, was one of the most shameful events in our history." The history of child labour is, thus, reduced to a chronicle of blighted childhood. McIntosh, in *Boys in the Pits,* reassesses this orthodoxy. In the first part, he examines "how changing attitudes and practices regarding childhood, class relations at the colliery, mining technology, the state, the working-class family, and the mining community shaped the world pit boys encountered. These circumstances drew boys into the mine, defined their place there, and eventually expelled them from the colliery." Children also laboured in sawmills, match factories, ropemaking, and bakeries across the country. Wherever new divisions of labour and machinery produced jobs that required little skill or strength, children were found employed.

The majority of the boys were taken into the mines by their fathers, brothers, or other relatives. The family claimed they were putting their sons into an apprenticeship. However, there were times when the adults were jealous of the boys because two boys were hired for each man. The men were also resentful of the boys, at times, because the boys were unionized and went on strike often. Many of the pit boys experienced accidents in the mine, including broken bones, and even death as a result of rock and coal falls, being crushed, working around underground transportation on mine slopes and traveling roads. The author notes, the root of the problem lay with careless individuals who made bad decisions. *Boys in the Pits* is well documented, with detailed footnotes and an extensive 37-page bibliography. It will be useful to labour historians interested in Canada, child labour, and the history of mining.

Selena Lai (edited by Sarah Bachman), 2001, *A Global Investigation of Child Labour: Case Studies from India, Uganda, and the United States,*[17] Three multi-part lessons built around detailed case studies of a street child in India, child soldiers in Uganda, and a migrant farm worker in the United States. Lesson One, "Understanding Child Labour," introduces child labour according to UNICEF definitions and includes a knowledge assessment activity, analysis of complexities associated with sample child labour cases, small group work constructing a slide show on a particular form of child labour, and a homework reading assignment. Lesson Two, "The Complexity of Child Labour," includes a "jigsaw" group activity in which students work together to present part of an assigned reading, a "team quiz" activity based on student-generated questions, and a homework writing assignment. Lesson Three, "A Closer Look at Child Labour: Case Studies from Around the World," provides three detailed case studies to be distributed in packets to small groups, along with materials for each group to use in analyzing and constructing a presentation on their case. This is a very dense curriculum that contains a high level of factual detail and nuanced reading material; lessons could each potentially fill over a week's worth of classes. Emphasis is on encouraging students to recognize particularities of each child worker's situation as well as the "universality" of issues many child workers face in common. Readings and contextual information consistently emphasize the complexities surrounding child labour issues and potential approaches to mitigating its harmful effects; accompanying activities place information on complicated, unresolved issues in front of students and ask them to generate possible responses and solutions. Curriculum includes multiple reproducible handouts, prepared and reproducible transparencies for use in instructor presentations and student group work, "information cards" with questions and factual answers for use in classroom discussion, homework cards with short assignments, and activity cards, worksheets, and scenarios/case studies for students to use in group work. Curriculum guide concludes with a 20-page resource section.

In *'Child Labour: An American History,*[18] *Hugh D. Hindman*, 2002, studies that despite its decline throughout the advanced industrial nations, child labour remains one of the major social, political, and economic concerns of modern history. The work presents the most comprehensive treatment of child labour in early twentieth century America, that has been published till date. The author first discusses child labour as a social and economic problem in America from historical and theoretical perspective. He then presents child labour as the National Child Labour Committee investigators found it in major American industries and occupations, including coal mines, cotton textile mills, glass manufacturing, street trades, and agriculture in the early 1900s. The investigators reports are supplemented by other government publications as well as on-the-scene photographs by Lewis Hine, a famous social photographer of the times. Finally, Hindman assesses child labour today, integrates these findings, and applies them to child labour problems in America and the world.

Hindman succeeds in presenting a portrait of working children that exposes the complexity of reform movements, the needs of industry, and the relationship to both to changing ideals and schooling, the family and the state. The book discusses American History as an important contribution to the scholarship addressing the relationship between seemingly solutions and the complex forces surrounding the work of children in any society. The book appeals to scholars in labour economics, law and economics and industrialization. It is infact more than just contemporary relevance that makes this study so attractive. Hugh Hindman has provided a much-needed survey of child labour....lively, insightful, and an excellent introduction to the topic.

Arun Kumar, 2002, in *'Child as Human Resource: Policies and Approaches,*[19] discusses the development of children as a task area of planning and management which has changed a lot at different points of the planning era in the contemporary times. Human resource development has to be an integral part of development planning so as to enable the poverty groups in rural areas to achieve a minimum level of living, a sense of belonging and opportunities for decision making in issues that vitally affect them. The author also mentions about the Sector Policy Paper on Rural Development of the World Bank which states that rural development is a strategy designed to improve the economic and social life of a special group of people, the rural poor. The book also highlights about the importance and need of early childhood education and care. Child labour and its problems and human resource development are discussed in the context of their relationship. Contemporary status of girl child in India and the measures for child development with different indexes are dealt in detail. Most importantly the author discusses the role of education and employment in child development in the light of various perspectives. A detailed discussion on the condition of urban children with relevant examples from the field is also included in the study.

Arun Kumar also attempted to present an account on the female foeticide in India and has discussed it in indexes of socio-economic dynamics. His study also divulges the status of women in patriarchal societies in India and also the existing legal provisions relating to female foeticide. Atrocities against urban children have been also studied in detail. The appendix section of the book study the various articles meant for safeguarding the interests and preserving the child from exploitation and abuse and also to prevent human rights violation with regard for the development of child community.

'Child Labour: How to Investigate'[20] by M.I. Siddique, 2003, sheds light on various concepts and notions concerning child labour. Some basic but important concepts have been explained, wherever definitions are not possible. Informal sector, for example, is the most talked about being the major provider of employment in any and every developing country but no satisfactory definition is available and thus, it has been explained. What is to be investigated forms the core of chapter two. Various aspects of child labour have been highlighted and explained. It is to identify some of the important themes in the field of child labour. But the exercise done in chapter two is simply indicative and suggestive. Then the author discusses about investigation methodology. It has been given stepwise so that the proper approach may be made. However, steps are based on logic only and not claimed as the 'hard and fast rules'.

In certain cases, child labour is of a 'hidden' nature, that is, not visible to everyone. These hidden traits also have some danger zones such as child trafficking, child prostitution and children under arms. Such unusual and hidden aspects can not be treated like wage-employment of children. Therefore, an effort has been made to provide some specific guidelines to investigate child labour in unusual spheres. The next chapter deals with report writing. It basically explains how to write a report? Report writing is technical and must have one or the other pattern required by the commissioning and or funding agencies and international organizations. The present manual explains report writing step by step so that the report is well organized and impressive. New comers in the field may find it quite useful. To sum up, Child Labour: How to Investigate, is an effort on the part of the author to create awareness and interest, among persons concerned, about the subject; its dimensions, concepts and research from the stage of formulation to the execution. However, the book is suggestive in nature and approach.

Analyzing child labour presents a number of problems discusses, *P. Anandarajakumar,* 2004, in *'Female Child Labour'.*[21] Children are major actors within the family and education system. They are also affected, both directly and indirectly, by specific socio-economic factors. In this regard, Dr. P. Anandarajakumar has covered a number of issues in this book by competently researching related aspects. The book reflects the outcome of intensive field work undertaken by the author. The efforts made by the author are worthwhile, significant and relevant for contemporary society. The author has tried to scan all the relevant and related studies and literature. He has also given a detailed introductory lesson about child labour in general and female child labour in particular. Methodology used in the study has been discussed in detail and studied in depth.

The strategies for human rights in India have identified in recent years the female child as a priority target focussed on her rights and status. This book presents vivid and penetrating analysis on the issue of female child labour. Whether it is the socio-economic background of child labourers, parental orientation towards female children's education and *beedi* works, production relations, personal and work profile of female child workers, economic contribution made by female child workers, perception of female child workers towards *beedi* works and education, recreation and health, etc. are discussed in detail.

The emphasis on gender dimension in the context of *'beedi'* rolling children is a unique one to be appreciated. Ultimately this book attempted to bring together the lessons and experiences learnt from the parents, child labourers, Non Governmental Organizations, Government Officials, trade unions and academics of repute. The model plan of action suggested by the author is a significant contribution of this research which deserves not only appreciation but also adoption by GOs and NGOs concerned.

'Small Hands in South Asia: Child Labour in Perspective'[22], by *G.K. Lieten, Ravi Srivastava and Sukadeo Throat, 2004,* is an outcome of the international conference held in Delhi on Child Labour in South Asia and is based on the essays by academicians, policy makers and activists, with varied perspectives on the issue. Considerable attention has been paid to evaluating the magnitude of child labour in South Asia, in particular in India. The considerably more liberal position treating all activities that interfere with schooling of children as labour is advanced in many of the essays. This line of reasoning emphasizes the importance of securing certain positive rights/freedoms such as the right to development, the right to education, and the right to childhood (these are enabling rights). In this context it is clear that securing certain privileged positive freedoms for the child should also ensure protection of his/her negative freedoms.

Attempts to identify the causal factors point to the limited explanatory power of income poverty, and bring out the importance of "generalized" deprivation as a determinant of child labour/work. Government intervention to remove malnutrition, to enhance access to drinking water, to create schooling facilities and to provide free education is emphasized as a means to ending child labour.

Sociological and demographic determinants of child labour have been studied: the consequence of high fertility and the social attitude towards child labour are identified as promoting labour market participation of children. The India, Pakistan and Bangladesh related case studies of child labour in industries such as match, carpet, glass bangles, diamond cutting and polishing, "bidi" and incense stick making, sack-stitching and prawn-peeling, garment industries provide vivid accounts of the "wretchedness" of child labour in these industries. The nimble finger (special skills) argument for the use of child labour has been dismissed. A case for compensating the loss in family income due to withdrawal of child labour is established.

Legislative state intervention is elaborately dealt with, and covers the ground of context, provisions, loopholes, impact, and enforcement. The insensitivity of the judiciary, the delays in judicial process, the onus of proof of age on the prosecution rather than on the accused, ambiguities in defining the authority to certify age, and inadequate personnel in the labour department are cited as important impediments to enforcing the various child labour laws. In a nutshell, the book is useful, but could have been better if the editors had resorted to the services of a professional editor.

The book *'Children, School and Work: Glimpses from India'*[23], by *G.K. Lieten, Anup K. Karan and Anoop K. Satpathy,* 2005, written on the basis of intensive fieldwork, shows in detail how the children have ideas about the world and about the adults. The authors have gone into eight villages and slum areas in different parts of the country and have documented what children are doing. By staying with the children, they have learned to look at the world through the eyes of the children and that is an existing experience. Altogether they have documented the childhood in around 2100 households and have thereafter closely followed 45 children for a couple of days and made a very detailed description of what they do and how they think.

The detailed picture of the daily lives of these children as they are represented in this book belies these views. Education is seen by them as an absolute necessity if the girl or boy wants to grow up as a normal citizen of this society. They learn to read and write and they learn good behaviour as well as new ideas. They learn ideas about gender equality, about secularism about health and environment. It is because of poverty and not because of wrong ideas that there is still a child labour problem. Both boys and girls throughout the day are collecting water, cleaning the house, looking after the cattle, cutting grass, looking after siblings, assisting in the shops of their parents. They fully cooperate in the social life of the family. All these children are active, they know their responsibilities and they help the family unit to function and to survive. For them it is part of growing up, of learning skills and of helping out.

'Children, School and Work: Glimpses from India' provides valuable insights which help to understand who these children are, what they are doing, how they are thinking, and thus also, how they can participate in a child centred development policies.

The work, *Globalization, Development and Child Rights,*[24]

2006, by *Kailash Satyarthi and Bupinder Zutshi,* is a collection of papers presented in keeping view with the issues discussed at the workshop entitled "Development, Destitution and Child Rights in the context of Globalization". The author identifies circumstantial evidence suggesting that child labour remains as an income generating necessity for poor families. Kailash Satyarthi presents paradigm of development and destitution and its impact on child rights. He extorts that development has failed to address the basic issues of hunger, illiteracy and diseases. The consequences of displacements have lead to distress migrations, which have directly affected basic human rights of children especially their education, health care and nutrition. The author explains the process of one way globalization and examines the existence of several laws but their tardy implementation and also provides judicial ways of combating child labour. The author presents in-depth study of agrarian crisis and child right violations and also provides insights into the food concerns for children. The work also gives a detailed description of links between urbanization processes and the phenomenon of trafficking of children for sexual exploitation. Bupinder Zutshi's study shows that there is no empirical evidence to indicate that globalization process has increased the magnitude of child labour in the country. His concern indicates that globalization process has arrested child labour decline in certain specific manufacturing industries while it has increased child labour in agricultural sector. According to the author the worst sufferers through globalization have been girls whose dropout rates from schools have increased and process of gradually weaning them away from education is gaining strength. In short, the author studies child labour in-depth, evaluates it through its causes and consequences, conditions of work, exploitative nature, effects on physical and mental health and also on social health through empirical studies in different fields of work at different periods of time. This study is a note worthy one as it has discussed child labour in connection with globalization and liberalization policies as these are said to be the biggest indicators of development in present day world.

The study by *C.K. Shukla and S. Ali, Child Labour: Socio-Economic Dimensions,*[25] 2006, presents the theme that the future of any nation depends upon the sound development of children. In order to construct a civilized, cultural and prosperous society the proper care and education of children is mandatory. Regarding the development of children there is an obstacle of one of the sensitive social problems i.e. child labour, which is to be eliminated and the rehabilitation of affected children is to be taken in a scientific way.

The authors have devoted their attention to existing situational analysis in India, its dimensions, legal and constitutional measures and protection envisaging the aspects that of health, working hours, education, wages, working places, hazardous effects, etc. to give a specific standard to the field of child labour. The emerging trends that of labour migration, and the dominance and linkage of trade and other economic activities have been explored in a society of industrially developing phase. The myth of economic necessity has been systematically analyzed to evade the myth and to put the children in an adoptive and rich learning and living conditions of social life. Further it has been described that how child labour affects overall human resource development in a particular society. Consequences of child labour on overall education and health have been posed as very critical. So it is exigent to acquire development in terms of education and health for overall welfare and development. The authors describe the socio-economic dimensions of child labour, their role in accelerating and checking child labour as different societies provide different perspectives and approaches. Various international regulatory authorities, civil societies and legislative measures have also been presented to come up with a balanced and systematic approach for the treatment of child labour. To sum up, the authors present very sensitive dimensions of child labour in India, and create the awareness and sense of realization so that an effective and balanced mechanism can be evolved collectively to counter the problem of child labour taking all the dimensions into consideration.

The work of *S. Wal, Combating Child Labour: Legal Approach*,[26] 2006, highlights the phenomenon of child labour, like all other social phenomenon, is historically and socially conditioned. Its emergence, growth and nature of dynamics are intrinsically bound with the changing trends in production and reproduction of a given social matrix. The author considers the socio-economic backwardness as one of the most crucial factors responsible for the rise and growth of child labour. The consequent unemployment, hunger, poverty and illiteracy forced the child to enter labour force. It would be pertinent to mention here that almost 73 per cent of the total child labour force in rural areas and urban unorganized sector are put under diverse forms of bondage by their own parents or guardians. Child labour is characterized by long hours of work, low remuneration, and exploitation.

The author points out that in the third world countries supply of the child labour is in plenty due to high birth rate and excessive immigration from rural to urban areas. It is quite evident that child labour is generally exploited on the basis of illegality involved in their employment as well as by undermining their productive capacity which includes their activity. The author signifies that child labour is a socio-economic problem which affects the development of children and it can not be abolished until poverty exists in the present form. There is an immediate need to improve the working and living prospects of working children. As the total abolition of child labour is not possible in short term, at least employment of children in hazardous occupations requires removal immediately. According to S. Wal the child labour problem is a global problem and requires redressel attention at global level from all nations particularly from societies where it is in abundance like India.

The work by *L.B. Punecha,* a Sociologist, *Child Labour: A Social Evil,*[27] 2006, highlights the institution of child labour as a global phenomenon and is quite pervasive over time and space. However, it is more concentrated in poor developing countries as compared to rich developed countries of the world. According to L.B. Punecha, inspite of all public pronouncements against the evil of child labour, India is today having the largest number of child workers in the world. Again, the evil is rising rather than declining, over time, especially in the case of female child workers. Most of the child workers come from poor families which can not afford to spare their children for schooling and make their children to work so as to augment their meagre family income which are otherwise insufficient for their survival. Most of these workers are concentrated in the unorganized sector of the economy comprising farm, forestry, livestock, carpet, handicrafts, fishing and other household industries where the productivity per person is low. Amongst the states, child labour varies between 9.70 and 0.79 in the case of male children, and between

7.29 and 0.25 in the case of female children. Andhra Pradesh had the highest incidence of child labour both for male and female children. Kerala shows the lowest incidence of male child labour, while Punjab has the lowest incidence of female child workers. The incidence of child labour is positively related with the level of poverty. It is strongly correlated with the level of illiteracy and the overall work participation ratio. The incidence is more in those areas which are not well developed both socially as well as economically. Hence the institution of child labour is essentially a case of under development, economic as well as social. These child labourers suffer in almost all walks of life whether it is their physical growth, mental or emotional growth, etc. Again this part of the world, i.e., South Asia gives place to the largest number of children in the whole world with pathetic life conditions. The author also provides some fruitful considerations in ameliorating child labour.

Child Labour from Different Perspectives,[28] 2006, a study by *Mahavir Jain and Sangeeta Saraswat,* both Economists, discusses child labour as a major impediment to economic progress. Child labour has direct relation with poverty, health, trade, education, employment and development. It needs lot of efforts not only from the Governments but from the society as a whole to tackle this problem. According to the author the issue of child labour began to emerge in the nineteenth century as a matter of concern in Europe and in the US. Child Labour is a pernicious practice, resulting in denial of the joy of childhood and access to education, which eventually impairs the personality and creativity of children, the evolution and growth of a full being. The plight and predicament of girl child, whether they are working at home or outside, is worse.

The child is compelled to shed sweat of brow to keep the wolf away from the door. In some families, when some disease or other forms of disability upset the delicate balance of the family budget, there may not be any alternative but to send the child to work. The income accruing from child labour may be a pittance but it plays a crucial role in saving the family from a shipwreck. Economic compulsions weighed heavily on the consciousness of poor parents that they would not mind colluding with the child's employer in violating the law and putting the child under risks of inhuman exploitations. Poverty and child labour thus always beget each other and tend to reinforce themselves.

C.K. Shukla and S. Ali, 2006, in their book '*Child Labour and The Law,*[29] discuss about the recently adopted United Nations Convention on the Rights of the Child (1989) affirms the right of children to education, self expression and freedom from exploitative work. Indeed the abolition of child labour was one of the guiding principles of the ILO's constitution in 1919, and it remains one of its child goals, studies the authors in the present volume in detail. The National Policy on Child Labour and The Child Labour (Prohibition and Regulation) Act, 1986 has been given a special touch in this study so as to come across the loopholes of the policies and regulations.

A cursory glance over the constitution of India by the authors would reveal that few relevant provisions relating to child labour as well as child welfare have been incorporated in Part Third and Fourth dealing with Fundamental Rights and Directive Principles of State Policy respectively. Special reference has been given of Dr. B.R. Ambedkar and other framers of the constitution who were quite aware about the problem of child labour and due to this reason a Fundamental Right in favour of children was incorporated by them in Article 24 and respectively, the employers were totally prohibited employing children below the age of fourteen years.

The present study discusses the various labour legislations, viz., the Factories Act, 1948; The Plantations Labour Act, 1951; The Mines Act, 1962; The Merchant Shipping Act, 1958; The Motor Transport Workers Act, 1961; The Shops and Commercial Establishment Acts of various States as well as Territories, etc., meant for safeguarding the interests as well as the welfare of the children under work. In almost all its forms child labour exists in the length and breadth of country both in rural as well as in urban areas. Shukla and Ali rightly make poverty and weak educational system in India responsible for the institution of child labour and its end results of exploitation and physical damage to children. In the end we can summarise that the volume is a valuable contribution particularly from the legal aspect point of view towards the institution of child labour.

Child labour is visible in most of the developing and under developed nations of world studies *Soham*, 2006, in his book entitled '*Child Labour*'.[30] Despite several legislations banning employment of children, this social malady is not resolved. This phenomenon is more prevalent in the unorganised sector. The basic reason for such an inhuman practice is poverty and lack of education. In India many industries employ child labour to save on costs and raise profits. The Government is no doubt doing something to prevent the abominable practice but the parents' poor economic conditions drive them to send their wards for work. Firstly the parents' concerns should be addressed by providing them a life with minimum basic needs. Then it might be possible for them to allow the children to go to school and get education. A mass campaign should be started in every part of the country deploring the practice of child labour and exhorting the poor parents on the need to get their children educated even if it required a certain amount of sacrifice. In conclusion the author wish the NGO'S start a movement in far flung areas to create the right kind of impact on the concerned to annihilate this practice of child labour.

Jamal Siddiqui, 2006, in '*Child Labour and Human Rights*'[31], highlights, that the magnitude of the child labour force may be considered as an indicator of economic development, political maturity and social order of a region or a country. The present study focuses on poverty which pushes a child into work and exploitative condition at an early age. However it is a widely accepted misconception that child labour is an unavoidable consequence of poverty, but it is true that child labour is mainly caused by poverty. The study studies the fact that employers employ children to save labour costs in production, which ultimately leads to profit maximization. Indebtedness among families especially rural agricultural is another cause for families to keep their children employed as domestic servants, agriculture workers. This is also one of the major causes for bonded labour. Another reason which the author highlights is that families of child labourers consider education as "time consuming" "money consuming" and "unproductive" exercise. The commercial sexual exploitation of children has become a global issue.

Non-Governmental Organizations have emerged to be a potent force in catalyzing various actions through the mobilization of social forces and pressing govt. to take needed action. The book discusses the issues before us today and how to find ways and means to eradicate the multiple forms of child abuse and neglect suffered by child workers.

The cost of making primary education universal is undoubtedly high, but cost of not having compulsory education is even higher and the highest cost is paid by children themselves. Participation of children in schools will reduce their participation in labour activities. And finally, the author conveys to the Governments political will to implement the guidelines of its own constitution as well as of international conventions on child rights, whereas international agencies should also pressurize Nations to implement the conventions.

In this accessible treatment of child labour in Africa, '*Annie Kielland and Morizia Tovo*, 2006, *Children at work: child labour practices in Africa*'[32], straight forward prose is enriched throughout with photographs that give a human face to the issues involved. The authors draw on sources ranging from scholarly studies to children's own voices. After providing a general background to the topic-debunking myths in the process-they describe the work typically done by African children in the home, as apprentices, and in commercial labour markets. They also present a clearheaded discussion of the worst, exploitive kinds of child labour. The book ends with a discussion of the effects of work on children, suggesting a variety of concrete, realistic approaches to minimizing negative consequences.

The book *'Childhood Regained'*[33], by, *Kalpana Sankar and Kalyani Rajaraman,* 2007, is about the growth of an NGO, one of the many in progressive Tamil Nadu. But essentially, it is about the children, the organization, *Hand in Hand*, serves and their compulsions to work for a living. The slim, well-produced book is rich with the experiences its two authors have gained working at the grass roots with children. The strength of the book is not only in its setting out an elaborate model that could be replicated elsewhere in India, but also in its human approach-outlining the stories of children with real problems. Be it 13-year-old Mariyamma from Amaravathy Patnam whose family had been bonded to a quarry owner, or Raja who was 'supposedly' possessed by the local deity, the stories are fresh, almost as if they have come right out of the dusty Kancheepuram villages right into the pages of the book. What is also commendable is the attempt not to romanticise a success story or gloss over the process of social transformation.

B.K. Sharma, 2007, in '*Socio-Economic Profile of Child Labour in a Developing Economy*'[34], writes that in the developing countries children work for subsistence whereas in the developed ones they work for pocket money. One of the unique characteristic of child labour is that employers consider it as source of cheap labour and measures of quick profits. Employers prefer children because they can be paid less and exploited more. Low wages paid to the children give them a competitive advantage not only in the national market but also in the international market. In rural areas the children of marginal farmers and landless labourers are generally found to be working in various agricultural operations right from their early childhood. They work as helpers during sowing, harvesting and threshing operations. Children from the families with little or no land are more likely to be in the labour market. There is positive relationship between the schooling of the child and age of entry in the employment. Child labour not only deprives the working children of the basic schooling and vocational training but also forces them into the ranks of unskilled workers who have to receive low wages throughout the working life. A study has found that the producers would like to stop production rather than hire adult workers because of great reduction in profits.

Although multifarious causes are responsible for a wide spread of child labour in the developing countries, the extreme poverty of the household is the main cause. Another important cause of child labour is the widespread unemployment among the adults from the lower income strata of population. Besides, inadequate, irregular or no family income is also responsible for child labour. UNICEF's criteria for child labour exploitation has also been discussed which included full time work at too early an age, too may hours spent in working, work that exerts under physical, social or psychological stress, work and left on the streets in bad condition, inadequate pay, too much responsibility, work that hampers access to education, work that undermines children's dignity and self esteem such as slavery or bonded labour and sexual exploitation, work that is detrimental to full social and psychological development.

D.C. Nanjunda, in the book *'Child Labour and Human Rights: A Perspective,*[35] discusses the recent trend in the global system for evaluating the development of any country not in terms of their military or economic strength or the splendour of their capital cities and big public buildings, but also in terms of human development or the well being of its citizens. Against this backdrop, the existence and perpetuation of child labour has been one of the main limiting factors standing in the way of human development in almost all the developing countries, including India. The issue of child labour is a worldwide phenomenon and it exists in almost all the countries of this planet. Meanwhile it is very sad to write that India is one among the nations in the world, which has the unique distinction of being a large employer of child labour. Since child labour is a more complex natured problem, a balanced approach is needed to solve this issue with an interactive role from all concerned people and the agencies. The author suggests that it is the right time for all to be highly and really think regarding ensure of better social, political and economic lives to all sections of the society, at least in the interest of human rights in this new millennium. Apart from the normal style, this book contains some thematic discussion on child labour and human rights. Each chapter written is based on grass root experiences of the author. That is the creamiest part of this book. Each and every chapter of this book gives a different outlook on the problem to the readers. This book is highly useful to academic people, anthropologists, policy makers, NGOs, research students, development agencies and others, interested in studying the growing problem of child labour.

REFERENCES

1. Sharad D. Gokhale and Neera K. Sohoni. 1979. *Child in India. Mumbai:* Sumaiya Publications.
2. S.K. Tripathy. 1989. *Child Labour in India.* New Delhi. APH Publishing Corporation.
3. Amarnath Singh. 1990. *Child Labour in India.* New Delhi.
4. Ramesh Kanbargi. 1991. *Child Labbour in the Indian Sub--Continent-Dimensions and Implications.* New Delhi. Sage Publications.
5. Indira Hirway, Jacqui Cottyn and Pushkar Pandya. 1991. *Towards Eradication of Child Labour: An International View.* New Delhi.
6. Nazir Ahmad Shah. 1992. *Child Labour in India.* New Delhi. Anmol Publications.
7. Jinesh C. Kulshreshtha. 1994. *The Child Labour in India.* New Delhi. Uppal Publishing House.
8. Varandani Gursharan. 1994. *Child Labour and Women Workers.* New Delhi. Ashish Publishing House.

9. Mittal Mukta. 1994. *Child Labour in Unorganized Sector.* New Delhi. Anmol Publications.
10. Kulshrestha C. Jinesh. 1996. *Child Labour in Indian: Lock Industry. New Delhi.* Uppal Publishing House.
11. G.P. Mishra and P.N. Pande. 1996. *Child Labour in Carpet Industry.* New Delhi. APH Publishing Corporation.
12. Airyn de Tenorio. 1998. *Child Labour in Domestic Service.* Geneva. Switzerland Bureau for Workers Activities. International Labour Office.
13. Francesco D'Adamo's. 1998. *"Iqbal".* Publisher Atheneum.
14. Marita Ishwaran (edited by Caroline D'Souza and Jaya Menon). 1999. *Violation of the Child's Human Rights: "Street Children," "Child Labour," and "The Girl Child".* Bombay. Research and Documentation Centre. Justice and Peace Commission. Asian Human Rights School.
15. Olga Niewenhuys. 1999. *Children's Lifeworlds: Gender, Welfare and Labour in the Developing World.* London. Routledge.
16. Robert McIntosh. 2000. *Boys in the Pits: Child Labour in Coal Mines.* Montreal. McGill-Queen's University Press.
17. Selena Lai (edited by Sarah Bachman). 2001. *A Global Investigation of Child Labour: Case Studies from India, Uganda, and the United States.* Stanford Program on International and Cross-Cultural Education (SPICE). Institute for International Studies, Stanford.
18. Hugh D. Hindman. 2002. *Child Labour: An American History.* Princeton University.
19. Arun Kumar. 2002. *Child as Human Resource: Policies and Approaches.* New Delhi. Sarup and Sons.
20. M.I. Siddique. 2003. *Child Labour: How to Investigate.* New Delhi. Deep and Deep Publications. Pvt. Ltd.
21. P. Anandarajakumar. 2004. *Female Child Labour.* New Delhi. APH Publishing Corporation.
22. G.K. Lieten, Ravi Srivastava and Sukadeo Thorat. 2004. *Small Hands in South Asia: Child Labour in Perspective* New Delhi. Manohar Publishers and Distributors.
23. G.K. Lieten, Anup K. Karan and Anoop K. Satpathy. 2005. *Children, School and Work: Glimpses from India. New Delhi.* Amsterdam. Institute for Human Development.
24. Kailash Satyarthi and Bupinder Zutshi. 2006. *Globalization, Development and Child Rights.* Delhi. Shipra Publications.
25. C. K. Shukla and S. Ali. 2006. *Child Labour: Socio-Economic Dimensions.* New Delhi. Sarup and Sons.
26. S. Wal. 2006. *Combating Child Labour: Legal Approach.* New Delhi. Sarup and Sons.

27. L.B. Punecha. 2006. *Child Labour: A Social Evil.* New Delhi: Alfa Publications.
28. Mahavir Jain and Sangeeta Saraswat. 2006. *Child Labour from Different Perspectives. New Delhi:* Manak Publishers.
29. C.K. Shukla and S. Ali. 2006. *Child Labour and The Law.* New Delhi. Sarup and Sons.
30. Soham. 2006. *Child Labour.* New Delhi.
31. Jamal Siddiqui. 2006. *Child Labour and Human Rights.* New Delhi. Deep and Deep Publications Pvt. Ltd.
32. Annie Kielland and Morizia Tovo. 2006. *Children at work: child labour practices in Africa.* US. Lynne Rienner Publishers.
33. Kalpana Sankar and Kalyani Rajaraman. 2007. *Childhood Regained.* Hand in Hand. Kancheepuram.
34. B.K. Sharma. 2007. '*Socio-Economic Profile of Child Labour in a Developing Economy'. Delhi:* Himalaya Publishers.
35. D.C. Nanjunda. *Child Labour and Human Rights: A Prospective.* New Delhi. Kalpaz Publications.

4

WIDER THEORETICAL FRAME ON CHILD LABOUR

The resurgent interest in child labour has been accompanied by a combination of new international conventions, new actors, new investment, new research, new information, new ideas, and expanded activity in a wide variety of developing country economic and social settings. One result of this recent movement is increased diversity of both thinking and action. Both the literature and meetings on child labour are now marked by vigorous debate in regards to a number of important issues. Even among recognized experts, both researchers and activists, there is wide and often heated disagreement even over such basic matters as what constitutes child labour, what causes it, how it affects children and society, and how best to deal with it. The diversity of viewpoints should be encouraged, and that the creative tension between them can, if constructively managed, generate more effective action and cooperation against abuse of children in and through their work.

A review of the 'child labour' literature and experience reveals four highly generalized lines of thinking that can be thought of as: (1) a labour market perspective, (2) a human capital perspective, (3) a social responsibility perspective, and (4) a child-centered perspective.[1] It is suggested that each of the most important positions now encountered in current national and international discussion of 'child labour' tend to fit into one of these perspectives more easily than any of the others, and can be profitably understood in that context. It might be noted in passing that the first two perspectives are of an economic orientation, while the latter two tend to emphasize social and cultural factors.

The Labour Market Perspective

This perspective, the dominant international paradigm of government child labour intervention for nearly a century, is fundamentally driven by mostly west cultural notions of childhood as properly a work-free period and by anxiety about the potential impact of child workers on adult labour markets. While concern about workplace hazards on children's health and development has also been a factor, and has even been emphasized in political rhetoric, policies and programmes generated under this conceptual framework have been designed primarily to separate children from work until at least mid-adolescence, rather than to make their workplace safer or more conducive to their development.

The 'labour market perspective' takes a particular view of children, envisaging them as essentially innocent, ignorant of the world and incompetent to fend off its evils or even to recognize their own best interests. They are depicted as helpless victims, or potential victims, dependent on protection and rescue by adults. This is primarily a modern Western notion of childhood that is historically and anthropologically unusual not only for the radical division it draws between childhood and adulthood, but also for valuing children's helplessness rather than usefulness, and artificially extending their dependency to an advanced age by deliberately delaying instruction in certain life skills essential to survive, make one's living, or raise a family (Zelizer, 1985; Boyden, 1997; Boyden *et al.*, 1998). Such a view of childhood leaves children free of responsibility and obliges adults to take decisions on behalf of the young that children, owing to their incompetence by definition, are deemed unqualified to take for themselves. There also is a built-in assumption that what is best for adults probably is good for their children as well.

The Human Capital Perspective

This approach views the work of children through the lens of national economic development. It regards child labour as a product of economic underdevelopment, and suggests that the remedy is to eliminate poverty and its causes. At the macroeconomic level this entails raising the Gross National Product, and at the microeconomic providing enhanced income options for the poor. It conceives of the child labour problem in terms of work and working conditions that undermine children's eventual contribution as adults to national economic development and their own economic progress, and makes no objection to children's work, per se. However, a "human capital perspective" would worry about work that stands in the way of children receiving an education, and for this reason economists and others working within it have produced a considerable literature looking at the relationships between children's work, education, and lifetime earnings. The interpretation of findings from literature, which appear ambiguous, is currently a matter of intense discussion. This perspective promotes policies and activities to develop in children the skills, attitudes and other capacities—the 'human capital'-they need to contribute to economic development and become prosperous adults. It judges children's work according to whether it contributes to or detracts from this objective, opposing work that deprives children of education, for example, but approving apprenticeships or other work arrangements that transmit skills.

The decision to educate one's children has an inter-temporal asset, as discussed by many authors, most notably Becker (1974). Baland and Robinson (2000) make a particularly direct connection of human capital formation to child labour when evaluating the efficiency characteristics of household decisions.[2]

The Social Responsibility Perspective

This perspective regards the work of children in the context of social rather than economic development. It arises out of concern about social inequality, many types of discrimination, unjust concentrations and use of economic and political power, cultural alienation, dysfunctional family and community relationships, social irresponsibility, and the deterioration of values and moral fibre. The central concern is with the 'exclusion' of disadvantaged groups from full participation in the protection, benefits and opportunities of society, and the proposed remedy is greater social inclusion of those being excluded or marginalized.[3]

The Child-Centered Perspective

Unlike the other conceptual frameworks discussed above, 'child-centered' interventions in child work have children as their primary clientele, putting their interests first and foremost without filtering them through prior adult agenda. Unsurprisingly, this perspective is most associated with organizations for the defence of children. It is prominently represented at the international level by UNICEF and international child rights organizations such as the Save the Children Alliance, and at the national level by a huge number of non-governmental and community organizations promoting children's rights and welfare. It is driven by concern about conditions that impair children's growth and violate their rights. Accordingly, it conceives of child labour as that work which undermines children's well-being and individual and social development, and it judges the appropriateness of any work according to its effect on a child. Work is broadly defined to include much more than economic participation; for instance, girls working in their homes are included in the focus. The purpose of intervention in children's work is to guarantee their rights, welfare and development.

Theory of Inequality, Productivity, and Child Labour

A recent theoretical literature has linked reductions in income inequality to reductions in child labour in countries that are relatively well-off, but has not explored how income distribution affects child labour in very poor countries. We show that while in higher-productivity countries with child labour, a more equal income distribution will reduce or eliminate child labour, in low-productivity countries, a more equal distribution of income will exacerbate child labour. Econometric specifications studying child labour among 10 to 14 year olds yield results generally consistent with these predictions. Policy actions that aim to bring about more equality so as to reduce child labour will likely not have the desired effect unless a country in which they are taken is sufficiently wealthy (Rogers and Swinnerton, 2001).

Karl Marx

The result of buying children and young persons of under age by the capitalist is physical deterioration and moral degradation. Karl Marx provided detailed brief for the General Council on social issues likely to meet with immediate agreement. Child labour was deemed such an issue. Marx's position on child labour as "a progressive, sound and legitimate tendency, although under capital it was distorted into an abomination' met with no opposition.[4] Marx believed that no child under nine years of age should work. He then divided older children into three age groups of 9-12, 13-15, and 15-17 years and suggested that they should be allowed to work two, three and six hours per day, respectively. Marx was a supporter of part-time education, and was sceptical about the role of the state in education (he had Prussia in mind).[5]

Theoretical Explanations of Child Abuse

A number of explanations have been given by scholars to explain the motivational factors in child abuse. Of these, the important ones are: (1) psychiatric explanation; (2) socio-cultural explanation which includes (a) social situational explanation, (b) social habitability explanation; (3) resource explanation; (4) social interactional explanation; and (5) social learning explanation.[6]

The psychiatric explanation was propounded by scholars like Kempe (1972), Steele and Pollock (1968), Gelles (1973), and Parke and Collmer (1975). It links with child abuse factors such as mental illness and personality defects or intra-individual abnormalities. It also links abusive parents' own childhood experiences to the individuals' weak personality development and poor self control (Wolfe, 1987: 45). The thesis that personality disorder is responsible for child abuse was further advanced by reports that abusers often had a propensity for impulsive and/or anti-social acts that extended beyond the preventive role. A parent, according to this explanation, may abuse his/her child due to unmet emotional needs (that signify discontentment, anger or irritability), an inability to balance the child's needs and capabilities with own (parental) expectations, or emotional scars from their ability to care for their own offspring (Wolfe, 1987: 45).

This explanation initially drew support from many fields, including law-makers and public-interest groups because it directed most of the responsibility for abusive behaviour squarely at the individual involved, and absolved society from blame in contributing to the risk of child abuse through lack of education, adequate housing, family support programmes, employment opportunities, and so on. However, recent researches have disproved the role of psychopathology in child abuse.

The socio-cultural explanation, given in the 1960s, maintained the external forces or socio-demographic variables within the society caused child abuse. This explanation includes three sub-explanations: social situational, social habitability and social control.

The social-situational explanation proposes that abuse and violence arise out of two factors: structural stress and cultural norms. As the social structure in which a parent lives becomes more stress ridden (or is perceived as more stressful), the greater becomes the possibility that family violence will surface as an attempt to gain control over irritating, tense events. Cultural sanctioning of violence as an appropriate conflict resolution technique further provides a foundation for the use of corporal punishment in child rearing. If a parent was frequently exposed to harsh physical punishment as a child, he/she may have greater propensity towards viewing such behaviour as normative and inhibition against physical force may be lessened (Bandura, 1973). Steinmatz and Strauss (1974) have maintained that factors such as low income, unemployment, isolation, unwanted pregnancy and conflict with spouse/in-laws, cause structural stresses which, combined with cultural acceptance against children at home.

The major problem in this explanation, according to Fieldman, (1982) is that it is unable to account for the finding that given the same set of deprivation or adverse conditions, many parents do and others do not abuse their children.

The social hospitability explanation was proposed by James Garbirino in 1977. According to him, the nature of child maltreatment depends upon the quality of the environment in which the person and family live, or the level of family support in the environment. The lesser the family support the greater the risk of maltreatment of children.

The social control explanation was propounded by Gelles in 1973.

According to him, parents use violence against their children. Violence is used when (1) the cost of being violent is to be less than the rewards, (2) the absence of effective social control over family relations decreases the cost (of one member being violent towards one another), (3) family structures reduce social control in family relations and, therefore, reduce the costs and increase the rewards of being violent (Gelles and Comell, 1985: 121). Gelles (1973) has maintained that certain types of children-like the handicapped, ugly, demanding, premature-are at a greater risk of being abused by their parents. This is because the parent perceives the cost of parenthood to outweigh the rewards; he uses violence against his children. Ivan Nye (1979) like Gelles, had also earlier accepted the application of Peter Blau's theory, in explaining child abuse. He has proposed that child beating is least common in families that have relatives and/or friends nearby.

The explanation has been criticized on the ground that: (i) It is preposterous to assume that relations between parents and children are based on reciprocity and that parents' treatment of children is determined in terms of calculations of rewards and costs. (ii) Assuming it is so, why do all the parents not make such calculations and only a few do it, that is, why do all the parents not beat their children and only some parents indulge in child beating?

The resource explanation was given by William Goode in 1971. According to it, the use of force by an individual depends upon the extent to which he can command or master the resources-social, personal and economic. The more resources a person has, the less he/she will use force in an open manner. Thus, a father who wants to be dominant person in the family but has little education, low prestige job, low income and lacks interpersonal-skills may choose to violence against his children to maintain the dominant position.

The social Interactionist explanation was given by Burgess in 1979. It approaches the etiology of child abuse in terms of the interplay between individual family and social factors in relation to both past (for example, exposure to abuse as a child) and present (for example, a demanding child) events. The parents' learning history, interpersonal experiences and intrinsic capabilities are regarded as predisposing characteristics presumed to be important contributors to an abusive pattern. In this explanation, the potential role of a child in provoking abuse is also acknowledged.

The interactional explanation, thus, is not necessarily limited to observable behaviour alone (like parental criticisms or displays of anger) but includes cognitive and effective processes too (like intelligence, attitudes) that may mediate behavioural changes.

Theoretical Models/Perspectives on Social Problems

Every science, including sociology, accumulates knowledge through interplay between theory and research. A theory is a set of statements that explains the relationship between phenomena. The key role of theories is to tell us why something occurred. They help us organize the data from research into a meaningful whole.[7]

As theory provides a point of view for the study of specific problems, an attempt is made here to introduce some of the relevant theories with the ultimate aim of applying them in the empirical data analysis and discussion.[8] Major theories covered are:

1. Structural Functional Theory;
2. Conflict Theory;
3. Exchange Theory;
4. Reference Group Theory;
5. Production Relations.

1. *Structural Functional Theory*

Structural functionalism has its family tree in the work of early sociologists, especially Durkhiem and Weber. Among modern-day scholars, it is most closely allied with the work of Talcot Parsons (1951) and Robert Merton (1968). It is leading theoretical view in sociology today.

The term "structure" and "function" refer to two separate but closely related concepts. Structure can be compared to the organs or parts of the body of an animal, and functions can be compared with the purposes of these structures. Like a biological structure, a social system is composed of many interrelated and interdependent parts or structures with specific functions.

Social Structures and Systems: Central to an understanding of social structures is the concepts of "status" and "role". Simply defined, a status is a socially defined position. Status is both ascribed and achieved. Sets of interrelated statuses of mother, father, and children, for example, constitute a family system.

Each social system performs certain functions that make it doable for society and the people who comprise that society to exist. Each serves a purpose that leads to the continuation or firmness of the larger society. The functionalist perspective assumes that these social systems have an underlying tendency to be in symmetry or balance; and system that fails to fulfil its functions will result in an imbalance or disequilibrium. In acute cases, the entire system can breakdown when a change or failure in any one part of the system frequently provokes changes elsewhere in the system.[9]

According to Merton, a social system can have both manifest functions and latent functions. Manifest functions are intentional and recognized; latent functions are neither intentional nor recognized. Merton recognized that not consequences of systems are functional-that is, they do not lead to the maintenance of the system. Some lead to unsteadiness or the collapse of a system. These consequences he termed dysfunctions. Robert Merton's theory of functional alternatives provides one way to avoid such dysfunctions. Functional alternatives are other ways to achieve the intentional goal.

2. *Conflict Theory*

The conflict perspective in modern sociology derives its brainwave from the work of Karl Marx who saw the struggle between social classes as the 'engine' of history and the main source of social change. Among its latest proponents are such people as Mills, Lewis Coser (1956) and Dahrendorf. They share the view that society is best understood and analyzed in terms of conflict.

Karl Marx began with a very simple assumption: the structure of society is determined by economic organization, predominantly the ownership of property. Inherent in any economic system that supports inequality are forces that generate revolutionary class conflict.

The browbeaten classes sooner or later recognize their submissive and inferior status and revolt against the dominant class of property owners and employers. In conflict theory, it is assumed that societies are in a continuous state of change, in which conflict is a permanent trait, "conflict" does not necessarily imply utter violence; it includes tension, competition and disagreement over goals and values.

Application of Conflict Theory

Conflict theory tells us to look for the hidden strains and frustrations, mainly between those in power who make the verdict by those involved does not mean the absence of conflict. Conflicting relationships is neither always explicit nor always expressed by individuals. The employees might not openly express their discontent because they may feel that they are powerless to change the situation. Infact, many sociologists have suggested that people fail to express dissatisfaction not because they feel powerless to change things, but they may not be aware that things could be better than what it is, or because they are resigned to the situation. However, there are some clues that could help one to recognize conflict.

Like structural functionalism, conflict theory is used by sociologists to (1) Explain the relationship between the parts of a social system and the inequalities that exist between these parts; (2) Discover and explain the sources of the conflict; and (3) Help create techniques to deal with conflict.

3. *Exchange Theory*

It is generally acknowledged to have been formulated by George Homans and developed by Peter Blau, with subsequent refinements by Richar Emerson and others.[10] This perspective is based on the belief that life is a series of exchanges involving rewards and costs. In economic exchanges, people exchange money, goods, and services, hoping to profit or at least break even in the exchange. Exchange theory assumes that people seek rewarding statuses, relationship, and experiences and try to avoid costs, pain and punishments. Given a set of alternatives, individuals choose those from which they expect the most profit, rewards, or satisfaction and avoid those that are not profitable, rewarding, or satisfying. When the costs exceed the rewards, people are likely to feel angry and dissatisfied. When the rewards exceed the costs, they are likely to feel that they got a good deal. Both parties are more likely to be satisfied with the interaction if there is perceived equity in the exchange, a feeling on the part of both the rewards were worth the costs.

Schools of Thought

There are two different schools of thought in the exchange theory perspective. George Homans believed that behaviour could be explained in terms of rewards and punishments. In exchange theory, the rewards and punishments are the behaviour of other people, and thus involved in exchanges assume that their rewards will be proportional to their costs. Peter Blau is the advocate of a different school of exchange theory. Blau argued that the exchange is more subjective and interpretative and that the exchanges occur on the symbolic level. As a result, money may be a just reward only if it is defined by the receiver as such, and psychic rewards of satisfaction with doing a good job or of pleasing someone may be as important as money, gifts, or outward responses of praise. Both agreed that all exchange involves a mutually held expectation that reciprocation will occur. If resources or exchange criteria are unequal, one person is at a distant disadvantage and the other has the control and power over the relationship. If there is indeed an imbalance of rewards and costs to one or all of the parties, then there must be some form of negotiation to restore the necessary balance of exchange.

Socialization of Norms and Values

Organizations engaged in exchanges are governed by their relative resources and by the norms of reciprocity and fairness. The society as a whole becomes stratified by the same kind of differentiation that characterizes its individuals. Overall solidarity is generated by "generalized media" of exchange: norms or laws, which codify the principles of exchange into abstract principles. Individuals learn these norms when socialized into society's system of common values. Possessions of these norms then make it possible for exchanges to take place at a distance, instead of through direct interaction.[11]

4. *Reference Group Theory*

George Herbert Mead had advanced a hypothesis that the individuals make self-evaluation and form attitudes only with reference to their membership groups, however, many theorists neglected the non-membership groups and failed to note that they too, like membership groups, have influence upon the attitude. Indeed they held a notion that individuals would be indifferent or hostile towards the non-membership groups but Merton notices that non-membership groups or out-groups also have influence on the individuals. In this connection, he has formulated a theory and the theory is known as reference group theory.

Merton says that both the membership groups are in-groups and non-membership groups are out-groups act as a point of reference for the individual for shaping his attitudes, evaluations and behaviour. But the membership groups are comparatively few, where as the non-membership groups are a legion. The later wield a greater influence upon the individual by acting as frames of reference in a number of matters. Further, Merton says that the individual generally tends to look up to his membership groups for evaluating his achievements, role performance and aspirations and ambitions. The membership groups provide contexts for the individual to compare with his associates and to make self-evaluation. But when the membership groups exert diverse and conflicting pressure for self-evaluation, the individual tends to adopt other non-membership groups as a frame of reference.

Functions of Reference Group

The reference groups serve two kinds of functions. (1) Set standard for the behaviours of the individual. The individual takes the standards and value judgments of the reference groups and shapes his attitudes and behaviour in accordance with them. Such reference groups are called as "normative" reference group and (2) provides a frame of comparison relative to which the individual evaluate himself and others. They provide a context for evaluating the relative position of the individual and others. Such groups are known as "comparative" reference groups.

5. *Production Relations*

The social relations which men enter into the course of producing material wealth of a society are fundamental, both in determining the structure of society and its development. The relations of production are the relations not between the human produce and nature, but between the human beings themselves as they occupy different places in society as a result of the division of labour, which is the basic character of human population.

According to Marx the relations of production form the economic structure of society. And this economic structure is the base not only for the other aspects of economic life, such as distribution and consumption, but also for the whole of the society with its other structures. Marx even identified the relations of the production with the relations of property as their legal expression.[12]

In Marxist theory, the mode of production can be defined as the labour process-forces of production, the relationship between the workers and the owners of the means of production, and between the workers and the product. Secondly, the mode of production is itself reproduced through the interactive process of economic, ideological and political mechanisms intrinsic to itself, and through its subordination of or by other modes of production. Thirdly, the mode of production embodies contradictions at each of these points which both drive it forward and develop the conditions for its own disintegration through the development of class struggle and of class alliance involving those enmeshed in the surrounding modes of production.[13]

Relations of exploitation or, to be more precise, the relations of surplus appropriation, are central to relations of production. This is the relation through which the immediate producers are alienated from the control of surplus of their labour.[14]

Using the Theoretical Perspectives

The major elements of each perspective and its view on social problems have been outlined in the following table. The perspectives should be seen as three different "tools", each of which is useful in analyzing particular social problems.[15]

Table 4.1: An Outline of the Sociological Perspectives

	Functionalism	*Conflict Theory*	*Interactionism*
View of Society	A system of inter-related and inter-dependent parts	Made up of groups struggling with one another over scarce resources	Individuals in face to face interaction create social consensus
View of the Individual	People are shaped by society to perform important functions for society	People are shaped by the position of their groups in society	People are symbol manipulators who create their social world through social interaction and consensus
View of Social Change	The social system tends to resist change as disruptive	Change is inevitable and continuous	Change occurs when there is no shared consensus about expected behaviour and newly found consensus develops
View of Social Problems	Caused by dysfunctional activities or disorganization in the social system	Arise when group believes its interests are not being served and works to overcome perceived disadvantage	Arise when a condition is defined as stigmatizing or disruptive of normal social expectations
Key Concepts	Integration, interdependence, stability, equilibrium	Interest, power, dominance, conflict, coercion	Interpretation, consensus, shared expectations, specially created reality

Constructing Social Problems

Use of the theoretical perspectives can be illustrated by looking at an important element of the study of social problems: how a social condition becomes a social problem. The existence of a condition alone, even when the condition produces negative consequences, does not make it a social problem; to become a social problem, it must be so defined by some group (Best, 1994; Holstein and Miller, 1993; Spector and Kitsuse, 1987). This process of social definition or construction involves a number of elements: how and why groups identify conditions as problems, how the groups develop an understanding of the causes of the problems, and how situations are developed and implemented. Each of the three perspectives contributes to our understanding of this process.[16]

From the *functionalist perspective*, the social construction of social problems depends, at least in part, on the extent of social disruption or social disorganization produced by a social condition. Conditions that are more disruptive are more likely to be defined as social problems by significant groups or large numbers of people. But many social conditions disrupt the lives of only some people, and these conditions may be defined as problems by some groups but not others.

The *conflict perspective* helps us recognize that elites and others with access to resources or power play a greater role in this process of social definition: it is the condition that negatively affect their values and way of life that are most likely to be defined as social problems. So, definitions of social problems are constructed out of the clash of competing interest groups.

The *Interactionist perspective* recognize the importance of symbols and social meanings in shaping human life, and it points out that defining a "condition" as a "problem" is a matter of attaching certain negative meanings to the condition. The process of interpretation is central to human social life, and people have to interpret a set of objective conditions as something that is 'bad' or 'negative' before they will act on it.

This brief illustration of constructing social problems demonstrates how using the three perspectives can provide a more complete understanding of a topic. This social construction process is complex and continuous, and the resulting social definitions are constantly shifting and changing.

REFERENCES

1. http://*www.spp.umich.edu*/rise/workingpapers/wp.html
2. D.K. Brown, A.V. Deardorff, R.M. Stern. 2002. *The Determinants of Child Labour: Theory and Evidence.* The University of Michigan; School of Public Policy. p. 9.
3. Myron Weiner. 1991. *The Child and the State in India.* Princeton: Princeton University Press.
4. Quoted in S. Padover (ed.). 1975. *Karl Marx on Education, Women and Children.* New York: McGraw-Hill. p. 91.

5. *Ibid.* p. 33.
6. Babita Agarwal. 2007. *Child Labour in India.* Jaipur India: ABD Publishers. pp. 110-114.
7. Thomus, J. Sullivan. 2000. *Introduction to Social Problems.* Fifth Edition: Allyn and Bacon. p. 9.
8. P. Anandarajakumar. 2004. *Female Child Labour.* Anmol Publications. New Delhi. pp. 20-26.
9. *Ibid.* pp. 20-26.
10. Randall Collins. 1997. *Theoretical Sociology.* Rawat Publications: Jaipur. pp. 338-348.
11. *Ibid.* pp. 338-348.
12. Bastiaan Weilenga. 1991. *Introduction to Marxism.* Bangalore: Centre for Social Action. pp. 26-27.
13. H.C. Srivastava and M.K. Chaturvedi. 1986. *Rural Middlemen-Network of Patronage.* New Delhi: Ashish Publishing House. p. 113.
14. B. Venkatesh Athreya *et. al.* 1990. *Barriers Broken-Production Relations and Agrarian Change in Tamil Nadu.* New Delhi: Sage Publications. p. 13.
15. Thomus J. Sullivan. 2000. *op. cit.* pp. 15-16.
16. *Ibid.* pp. 15-16.

5

RESEARCH METHODOLOGY

The Problem

"Child is the father of man" is an oft-quoted line from the poem of the famous English poet Wordsworth. Its real value has been realized only recently when the UNO and its various members have initiated programmes for the overall development of child population. This new trend has automatically drawn attention of the social scientists to the problems of growing children. Childhood has been considered as a most important period of life. During this period moulding and shaping of life takes place and the behaviour, conduct and sentiments are developed. Infact, the behaviour pattern, attitude and knowledge which are formed in the childhood of a person are never lost. As such, it is obligatory on the part of parents to educate their children. The future human resource of any country is thus dependent upon children of that country. The quality of the child is dependent upon various factors like services, rearing practices and problems hindering their growth and development. One such acute problem is the increasing incidence of employment of children in various jobs including hazardous and strenuous ones.

The employment of children has given rise to a number of social, psychological, economic and legal problems. Social evils involved in the employment of children are widespread dropout resulting in lack of development of child's personality which may continue even in his later life and other social disorganizations. The economic problem involved in the employment of children in handicrafts work and agricultural activities and cattle and sheep rearing, etc. are in no way less significant. The inadequacy of the family income and to fulfil personal needs etc. compel children to work in handicraft centres and agriculture. However employment in such establishments does not provide them with adequate wages. The legal problems involved in the employment of children in handicrafts work and agriculture, etc. are: (1) what should be their minimum age (2) what should be the industries in which they may be employed (3) what should be the nature of their work (4) what privilege should be afforded to them in matters of leave and holidays (5) what should be their duration of work (6) what protection should be afforded to them in matters of health, safety and welfare.

Agriculture, handicrafts work and traditional occupations have engaged a large chunk of the child workers in Kashmir valley. It is observed that around eighty per cent of the child labour force is still engaged in rural areas. In rural areas, children take up occupations as per the geographical and traditional requirements. It is because children still constitute a large labour force of handicraft sector particularly in the unorganized sector. Like in other areas, the working conditions of the children in the handicraft sector are deplorable, inhuman and uncongenial for the proper growth and development of the children. Various socio-economic, geographical and demographic factors are responsible for such a high proportion of child labour in India. Cheapness of the child labour in the agricultural and handicraft sector in Kashmir has led to the availability of the child labour in abundance. This has also resulted in their low level of schooling and a greater number of dropouts.

The employment of children in India in various sectors is quite widespread and common. Their working conditions are also very unsatisfactory, especially in the unorganized sector, where they have to work in ill-ventilated, ill-lighted, congested and dirty atmosphere. The inhuman aspect of the problem of the child labour has been attracting the attention of social scientists, states and central governments from time to time. The reports of different groups and bodies do mention the problem of the child labour and their treatment is often casual and limited in scope. A number of surveys conducted on the child labour do not present an integrated picture of the problem. As there is an increasing tendency to view the child labour as welfare approach rather than purely economic orientation, no study of this nature has so far been carried out in the vale of Kashmir. The present study is basically an attempt to fill up this gap.

The present study is of enormous significance on the following grounds:

1. Children are the most valuable asset of any nation and mankind owes to the child the best it has to give.
2. Fundamental rights and the directive principles of state policy adumbrated in the constitution of India which prohibits employment of children below fourteen years, protects the tender age of children from abuse, forbids their exploitation and ensures justice and human conditions.
3. Children are engaged in various types of employment and a considerable number are engaged in handicrafts work, as agricultural labourers, etc.
4. Children employed in the various occupations are very badly exploited not only by an employer but by parents as well. The work and the working conditions qualitatively as well as quantitatively are harmful, injurious for their proper physical growth and mental, intellectual and emotional development.
5. Since Kashmir is known for its handicraft items like carpets, embroidery, shawls etc, the demand of these items in the local as well as outside market require the production of these items. Employers prefer to employ children due to various reasons such as easy availability, cheapness, tender fingers for sophisticated work, easier supervision, lesser employee-employer's problem, etc. A significant number of children are employed in the handicraft sector in performing different types of work.
6. Despite the pitiable conditions of the children employed in the handicraft sector and agriculture etc, and the government efforts to protect them from exploitation, their parents are very keen to engage them in these occupations for narrow and short gains.
7. Though there is abundance of research studies on the child labour in general but, no sincere efforts have been made so far to study the child labourers/workers in the handicrafts and agricultural work etc, in particular from sociological point of view.

Definition of the Terms Used

Since there is a lot of dispute regarding the age range of the child as revealed by various State and Central as well as by different studies on child labour. The child worker is a person in the age group of six to fourteen years engaged in mental and physical work, in full time employment for the sake of reward or remuneration of earning at one's own house or at employer's working centre without any scope of attending school. The term child labour and child worker have been used interchangeably in the study. It is a matter of common knowledge that no child below the age of six years can take up paid employment due to his tender age. No employer will also like to employ them for obvious reasons. Though the upper age-limit varies in different Countries and Acts, the age of fourteen years subject to certain conditions is the minimum age required to work anywhere in any sector. Hence, the researcher has also fixed the upper age limit at fourteen years.

Magnitude of the Problem

According to one estimate children constitute around thirty percent of the world's population. An estimated two hundred and eighteen million children aged five to seventeen years are engaged in child labour, excluding domestic labour. Some one hundred and twenty six million of these children are engaged in hazardous conditions, such as working in mines, industries, chemicals, with dangerous machinery and in agriculture. They are everywhere visible, taking as domestic servants in homes, labouring behind the walls of workshops, hidden from view in plantation.

Millions of girls who work as domestic servants especially are vulnerable to exploitation and abuse. An estimated 1.2 million children are trafficked, forced into debt bondage or other forms of slavery (5.7 million), into prostitution and pornography (1.8 million) and other illicit activities (0.9 million). However, the vast majority of child labourers-seventy percent or more-work in agriculture (ILO).

Regional estimates indicate that:

1. The Asian and pacific regions harbour the largest number of

child workers in the five to fourteen age group, 127.3 million in total, (nineteen percent of children work in the region).

2. Sub-Saharan Africa has an estimated forty eight million child workers. Almost one child in three (twenty nine percent) below the age of fifteen works.
3. Latin America and the Caribbean have approximately 17.4 million child labourers (sixteen percent of child labour in the region).
4. Fifteen percent of child work in the Middle East and North Africa.
5. Approximately two to five million children are working in industrialized and transition economies. Children under fourteen constitute around 3.6 per cent of the total labour force in India. Of these children, nine out of every ten work in their own rural family settings. Nearly eighty five percent are engaged in traditional agricultural activities. Less than nine percent work in manufacturing, services and repairs. Only about 0.8 per cent works in factories.

Objectives of the Study

The main aim of the present work is to study the working and living conditions of child workers in the handicrafts, agriculture, streets, domestic work sectors etc, especially the situational factors forcing them to take up work at a particular age, their present working conditions, relationship with employers, existing legal protection and welfare provisions, vis-à-vis their implementation, health conditions, as well as perception of the child labour. The objectives of the study are as follows:

1. To make a detailed study of child labour in the handicraft sector, agriculture, hotels and restaurants, streets, etc, with special reference to their life conditions in Kashmir.
2. To assess the nature of exploitation faced by the children involved in labour activities.
3. To explore the causes of child labour working in the various sectors in Kashmir.
4. To examine the social implications of child labour in Kashmir.

5. To suggest the measures for ameliorating the child labour in the different sectors of the economy.

Hypotheses

On the basis of the earlier studies, personal observations, discussions with intellectuals and available reports on child workers, certain hypothesis were framed to be tested by this study. These hypotheses are as follows:

1. The existing conditions of these child labourers reveal that they suffer in all fields especially education, health, income, diet, hygiene, and working conditions.
2. State has done little to safeguard the interests of these children.

Universe

The universe of the study, handicraft sector etc., of Kashmir is well known all over the state, country and world. Jammu and Kashmir is situated between 32.17 degree and 36.58 degree north latitude and 37.26 degree and 80.30 degree east longitude. The total area of the State is 222,236 sq. kms including 78,114 sq kms under the illegal occupation of Pakistan and 42,685 sq kms under that of China. The State is bounded by Pakistan, Afghanistan and China from the West to the East. The State is well connected with rest of the country by air, rail and road. The state of Jammu and Kashmir is divided into 14 districts-Anantnag, Baramulla, Budgam, Doda, Jammu, Kargil, Kathua, Kupwara, Leh, Poonch, Pulwama, Rajouri, Srinagar and Udhampur. Jammu and Kashmir's economy is mostly dependent on farming and animal husbandry. Majority of the population of the state depends on agriculture. Paddy, wheat and maize are the major crops. Barley, bajra and jowar are cultivated in some parts. Gram is grown in Ladakh. Though small, the manufacturing and services sector is growing rapidly. Tourism formed an important part of the Kashmiri economy. The Wood in Kashmir is also used to make quality Cricket bats and as they are popularly known as Kashmir Willow. Handicrafts from Jammu and Kashmir have demand from both inside and outside the country. Coal, gypsum, and limestone are the major minerals produced in the state. Jammu and Kashmir is the only state where education is free up to university stage. Seasonal schools have been opened for people in the hilly areas and for the scheduled castes. Yet the state is educationally backward. Against the national literacy rate of 75.96 per cent for males and 54.28 per cent for females, the state has a literacy figure of only 65.74 per cent for males and 41.82 per cent for females respectively.

Sampling

In the present study, multi-stage sampling was used. In the first stage one block of every district of Kashmir (e.g. Qazigund from Anantnag, Khansahab from Budgam, Kakapora from Pulwama, etc.) was selected because of:

1. Concentration of more handicraft centres.
2. Employment of a large number of children in the handicrafts work, agricultural work and in other sectors.
3. Easy accessibility.

In the second stage fifteen percent villages/mohalas were chosen which included three villages/mohallas from every block for the study. All the villages/mohallas were arranged in serial order and thereafter every nth village/mohalla of every block was tick-marked and thus the villages/mohallas were selected out of the total number of villages for obvious reasons. The reasons mentioned above for the selection of the blocks were also kept into consideration while selecting the villages/mohallas. The decision of taking fifteen percent sample was decided after considering all the aspects and that this fifteen percent was considered to be a fairly good representative sample of the total villages/mohallas of the block.

In the third stage, a list of the working children in the handicrafts, agriculture, domestic work, etc. was prepared with the help of key persons, employers, senior citizens, and other knowledgeable persons. The sample was drawn out of the total number of children by using systematic sampling technique. Only two hundred child labourers could be interviewed in all the districts of Kashmir valley for various reasons. Care was also taken to interview at least one child worker from one family and to give due representation to all the dominant sectors wεre children are working. As per the objectives of the study, parents and employers too were selected using the same method. Seventy parents/heads of the households and thirty five employers were enlisted in addition to that. Also thirty five government officials and social workers/notables were interviewed for the present study. For statistical and other reasons, three hundred and forty respondents were interviewed only which include child labourers, parents, employers, social workers/notables and government officials.

Tools of Data Collection

Various tools for data collection are available for researchers. Suitability of these tools was examined for the present study. After discussion with the experienced researchers and the experts it was decided that the following tools would be suitable for the present study. These are:

1. Interview schedule
2. Observation
3. Collateral contacts
4. Interview

Since it is an empirical study, subjects of the study were to be interviewed for getting the relevant information as stipulated by the objectives of this study.

1. *Interview Schedule*: A schedule is a series of questions pertaining to the variables to be explored and described by the study. It is always useful to have a detailed list of questions to guide the interviews instead of depending upon memory. Schedule gives an opportunity to explain the questions and elicit the desired answers. It also helps in putting the questions more systematically and in the required order. In view of these reasons, a schedule was used to collect information for the present study.

2. *Observation*: We are aware of the limitation of the words. How the words are pronounced and the facial expressions of the respondents are extremely important to understand the communication adequately. This is possible only when the researcher note down his

observation along with words uttered by the respondents. Many things which can not be said are expressed bodily which can be observed and noted by any one. It is only for these reasons that observation has been used to supplement information collected through the interview schedule. Observation was very useful for collecting information about the facilities available to the respondents in their work units and their home conditions. These observations were noted in the research diary for use in the analysis of data.

3. *Collateral Contacts*: Collateral contacts were also used to supplement and corroborate the information. In this process, the researcher contacted neighbours, village heads, elderly and educated people of the village and co-workers of the respondents and the relevant information was noted down.

Collection and Analysis of Data

Plan of data collection was formulated to have more reliable information and responses to various questions. To start with, as planned earlier, the researcher went around the village and town and met various important persons including the masters/owners of the working centres to collect the basic information. The purpose of the study was explained. For the convenience of the respondents, as and when required, the objectives were clarified to allay their fear and suspicion. A research diary was also used to take care of those responses which were not in purview of interview schedule. Observations were noted and the interviews terminated with the acknowledgement of gratitude for their cooperation.

After collecting information from the field, the schedules were edited and rechecked in order to put all the information in proper and suitable order. Statistical calculations such as aggregation, percentage, average, mean, etc. were made in order to present the findings accurately. An attempt was made to establish relationship between different variables such as age, sex, education, religion, occupation, income, etc. Data was analyzed/interpreted systematically with logic and in the light of the facts of other studies.

Limitations

Since the units of the sample were widely scattered, so we couldn't afford to take a large sample because of time constraints, we decided to have a sample of limited villages and towns only. Thus, its findings can not be generalized and a similar study on a wider scale is needed. Despite the best effort made by the researcher to establish purposive rapport, it is easier said than done. The researcher also faced problem while travelling from one village to another due to absence of proper transport facilities. It is note worthy that the employers were quite apprehensive of the interviews as they considered the researcher as a government official deputed for collecting information about the abuse of child labour in different sectors of the economy.

It was difficult to get adequate answers from the children as most of them were immature and could not follow the questions. Moreover, fear and anxiety compelled them to remain silent which led to incorrect answers in many cases. Much has to be elicited, therefore, through observation. The researcher always tried to eschew the perceived notion which may mis-represent the findings. Some of the parents hide the information that the child was not an earning member but tried to pose that they send the child to work so that he may not be a victim of any anti-social element.

6

CHILD LABOUR IN KASHMIR

This chapter deals with the analysis and discussion of primary data collected from the study area. Children are engaged in various vocations and face a lot of problem at the workplace. They are exposed to extreme working and living conditions. In order to testify and verify the facts relating to child labour in the valley of Kashmir sociologically, we selected different areas for investigation. Accordingly, the present chapter focuses on the employment of child workers and their socio-economic characteristics viz., personal information of age and sex, education, occupation, family background, income, housing and working conditions, health conditions, etc. The tables in the chapter are presented logically by merging relevant variables in consonance with the objectives of the study. Percentages and averages are widely used to analyze the available data and accordingly interpretation is made.

Age and Sex Composition

Our first query to the child workers was regarding their age and sex. Age is an important factor which shapes one's personality and enables one to determine the work responsibilities and occupation one wishes to join for economic interdependence. So far as the age of child workers is concerned, for the present study, we chose the children between the age group of 6-14 years. Table 6.1 shows the age and sex-wise classification of child workers.

As different studies from different countries have already shown, the majority of child workers are male. This observation is confirmed in the findings of this study conducted in the different districts of

Table 6.1: Age and Sex Wise Classification of Child Workers

S. No.	Age Group	No. of respon-dents	Percen-tage	Sex	No.	Percent age
1.	7 to 10 years	54	27.00	Male	130	65.00
2.	11 to 14 years	146	73.00	Female	70	35.00

Source: Field study 2009.

Kashmir valley, where about two-thirds of the child workers are boys and only one-third are girls. The table 6.1 shows that majority of child workers were between 11 to 14 years of age. However, many children start work at an earlier age. It is a traditional pattern to pass on work knowledge from one generation to the next. Children join their parents or other relatives in their occupations when they are still very young. For, many of them, this means that they have never had access to education. They start their working career at the time they should enter school enrolment.

Overall analysis of population composition and their social position indicates that female population outnumbered male population, and they represent a potential source of labour in the handicraft sector of the economy. Further it is revealed that handicrafts work is female specific, especially at the household level leading to easy entry of female children in such an employment.

The Table 6.1 indicates that in Kashmir there are 65 per cent (130) male child workers and the female child workers are 35 per cent (70). This difference in the percentage was due to the fact that the female child workers were not involved in all types of work which we chose for this study. Most of the girls especially the ones engaged in handicrafts work were staying with their parents and in all these activities, their mothers were also engaged. But in some cases of female child domestic workers, very few of them were staying with their owners/employers.

Religion

The religious identity of respondents is presented in table 6.2. It is seen from the table that a vast majority of them are Muslims who constituted 97 per cent followed by Hindus whose concentration to the total sampled child workers interviewed is three percent. It is leant from the field that child workers in different sectors are mostly confined to Muslim community. It is taken up as a convenient and a better avenue of employment by all sections of population of the Muslim community. Muslims are also predominant in the constitution of population in Kashmir valley.

Table 6.2: Distribution of Respondents according to Religious Identity and Residence

S. No.	Reli-gious	No. of Respon-dents	Percen-tage	Residence	No. of Respon-dents	Percen-tage
1.	Muslims	194	97	Rural	126	63
2.	Hindus	6	3	Urban	74	37
	Total	200	100		200	100

Source: Field Study 2009.

Educational Information

Education plays an important role in one's life in the sense that it helps in shaping the right kind of life style in the human beings. It is education which turns children into a social and human being. Education formal or informal aims at developing the positive quality of the child and helps the individual realize his potentialities. Accordingly, we asked the child workers to state their educational qualification/background. Table 6.3 shows the educational status of the working children.

It is evident from the table that out of 200 sampled working children only 186 (93%) have been to school anytime and out of this 91 (48.92%) had education upto primary level, 72 (38.70%) upto middle and 17 (9.13%) had above middle attained education. Fourteen (7%) of the sampled child labourers were uneducated. It is disheartening to note that out of 186 (93%) working children who had attended school at any time, 143 (76.78%) were dropouts or had left school for good. Of this, maximum number of them became dropouts after primary education and some after middle education i.e. they could not complete their high and secondary education. Some child labourers 43 (23.11%) were still attending school but by observation it looks they too will leave the school in near future. In

Table 6.3: Educational Qualification of Child Workers

S. No.	*Attended school anytime*	*No. of Respondents*	*Percentage*	*Still Attending School*	*No. of Respondents*	*Percentage*
1.	Yes	186	93.00	Yes	43	23.11
Upto which class				No	143	76.78
(a)	Upto primary	91	48.92	Reasons for leaving school		
(b)	Upto middle	72	38.70	(a) Poverty	99	69.23
(c)	Above middle	17	9.13	(b) Lack of interest in school	27	18.08
2.	No	14	7.00	(c) No school available in locality	24	16.78
				(d) failed and then left	33	23.07
				(e) Parents sent to work	61	42.65
				(f) lack of quality education	67	46.85
				(g) Large family	19	13.28

Source: Field study: 2009.

order to stop this drop out rate there is a need to provide vocational education to all the working children after they complete their primary education.

Family Background

In the present study, the family is treated as a unit of analysis. Therefore analysis pertaining to the type of families prevails upon in the study area certainly throw some light on the issue of child labour. In general, it is believed and experienced that children in a joint family system would be given all protection and they would be facilitated to seek better education, recreation and the broader requirements of socialization itself. A critical look at the studies on child labour in the Indian context would reveal that disintegration of joint family system especially in rural society paved the way for emergence of child labour practice. It is equally true in the present study also. Data depicted in table 6.4 shows that nuclear families constitute 69.8 per cent to the total families child labourers belong to, followed by joint family which is 30.2 per cent. The table given below gives the details.

Table 6.4: Distribution of Respondents according to Type of Family and Strength

S. No.	*Type of Family*	*No. of Respon-dents*	*Percen-tage*	*Family Strength*	*No. of Respon-dents*	*Percen-tage*
1.	Nuclear family	139	69.5	Upto 5	34	17.00
2.	Joint family	61	30.5	Upto 8	48	28.00
				Upto 10	70	35.00
				Upto 15 and above	40	20.00
	Total	200	100		200	100.00

Source: Field study 2009.

Occupation of Parents (Father, if Alive)

Another related query was regarding the occupation of parents' i.e. father only. On the basis of the data which we collected, one can say that the parents were in those professions which could hardly provide two square meals to the family. The child workers families in rural areas were mostly working on the fields. Here they added that both the parents were working on the fields. Some of the male members in the families particularly in urban areas were found engaged in auto driving, selling fruits and vegetables, working in small factories and also as casual labourers. The below mentioned table gives a detailed statistical account of occupation of father and living parents.

Table 6.5: Distribution of Parents according to Their Occupation and Aliveness

S. No.	*Occupation*	*No.*	*Percentage*	*Parents alive*	*No.*	*Percentage*
1.	Farming	82	41.0	Father alive	8	4.0
2.	Unskilled labour	52	26.0	Mother alive	24	12.0
3.	Skilled labour	26	13.0	Both alive	158	79.0
4.	Business	9	18.0	Both dead	10	5.0
5.	Private Job	7	14.0			
6.	Govt. job	4	8.0			
	Total	200	100.0		200	100.0

Source: Field study 2009.

Thus we see that the occupation of child workers parents range from working on fields, casual labourers (skilled and unskilled), etc. to domestic help and private/govt. job. We at the same time asked the respondents about the parental employment i.e. whether both the parents are working or none is working. The chart 6.1 gives the detail.

Chart 6.1: Parental Employment

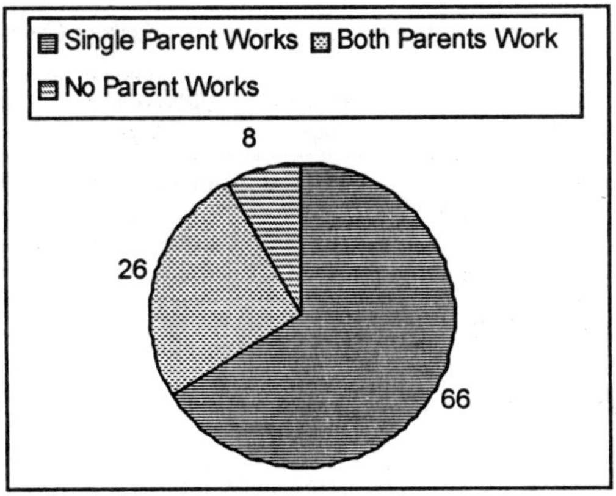

Unemployment is a big problem among child workers families. In most families' only one parent (60%) and no parent was employed in the families of 8 per cent child labourers. Cases were both parents are working are rare (11%). Females in Kashmir valley have a greater work load, in terms of total working hours, than males. This especially applies to non-market activities. The women also spent more hours than men in the informal sector. The women's contribution to the family income is increasing, however, at the same time; women continue their unpaid work caring for the family, the home, and the farm. In the families of the child workers, more fathers than mothers were employed.

Education of Parents

Most of the parents of the sampled child labourers were illiterate (74%) and only 26 per cent of child labourers were having their parents educated. Among the educated parents 68 per cent had received education upto primary level, 27 per cent upto middle and only 5 per cent had education above middle. The data clearly shows that there is a deep relationship between education of parents and child labour. The less the education of parents, the more are the chances of having working children and the more the education of parents, the less are the possibilities/chances of having children in work. The Table 6.6 shows it statistically.

Table 6.6: Education of Parents (Father Only)

S. No.	*Father Educated*	*No.*	*Percen-tage*	*Upto which Class*	*No.*	*Percen-tage*
1.	Yes	52	23.0	Upto primary	136	68.0
2.	No	148	74.0	Upto middle	54	27.0
				Above middle	10	5.0
	Total	200	100.0		200	100.0

Source: Field Study 2009.

Occupation of Child Labourers

In the valley of Kashmir children pick up any work that is near to their place of residence. Their parents, relatives and friends were the main motivators for them to undertake certain types of work responded 63, 21 and 16 per cent child labourers respectively. Table 6.7 presents the various categories of occupations of the children in which they were involved.

Table 6.7: Classification of Child Workers on the Basis of Types of Work

S. No.	*Type of Work*	*No. of Respondents*	*Percentage*
1.	Carpet weaving	46	23.0
2.	Agricultural work	34	17.0
3.	Hotel and Restaurant work	32	16.0
4.	Transport work	30	15.0
5.	Domestic work/help	32	16.0
6.	Shawl bawfi	26	13.0
	Total	200	100.0

Source: Field Study 2009.

The Table 6.7 depicts that children are engaged in almost all types of work.

Place of Work

After getting the details about occupation and arrangement of job, we asked the child workers the place/area where they are working. We got a mixed response because of which we could not present a tabular analysis of the data. Their place/area of work was scattered. But nevertheless, the majority (47%) of children works at employers' home/unit/centre and some (21%) of the child workers were working at home.

Working Hours

The work children are doing consumes considerable amount of time available at the disposal of children. As per the law, children should not work for longer hours. But in practice the law is not strictly followed. When we asked the child labourers about their daily working hours, they gave a mixed response which is presented in Table 6.8.

Table 6.8: Daily Working Hours of the Child Workers

S. No.	*Daily Working Hours*	*No.*	*Percentage*
1.	4 to 6 hours	30	15.0
2.	6 to 9 hours	86	43.0
3.	9 to 12 hours	78	39.0
4.	12 hours and more	6	3.0
	Total	200	100.0

Source: Field study 2009.

The Table 6.8 indicates that irrespective of occupation majority of child workers were found to work on an average more than 9 ½ hours of work every day. We were surprised to note that none of the children had normal working hours of less than four hours a day. Those children, who were self-employed i.e. working on their own, were in an advantageous position in the sense that their working hours were flexible. Whenever, they wanted to earn more money, they used to work for a longer time. Children falling under this category were mostly handicraft workers particularly females. On the other hand, those children who were employed by some other person were the sufferers in the sense that their working hours were neither fixed nor flexible. Even if they worked for longer hours, they were not paid extra for that work.

Duration of Present Job

Through statistical information it becomes clear that 76 (38 per cent) child workers were in the present job since last one year followed by 66 (33%) of who were in this occupation since last two years. About 17 (9.5%) of child labourers were in this business since last three years and the least number 24 (12%) were in the present job from last 5 years. The first category of child workers i.e. 38 per cent were those children who were engaged in handicrafts work, agriculture and domestic work. Thus, it can be said that there are certain vacations in which children continue to work for a longer period.

Interest in Work

Apart from willingness to continue with the present employment by the children, their liking towards their work is also studied and the reasons for liking and disliking are presented in table 6. 9.

It is noted that, inspite of all pervading exploitation and hazardousness with which children are working, they liked their work. Discussion held with both the parents and child workers revealed that they like it specially handicrafts and domestic work, since it is carried out conveniently within the houses and it does not require any physical risk unlike other occupations. Therefore it is inferred from the analysis that inspite of disliking and unwillingness, children are expected to work in different sectors of the economy to supplement the family income and also as matrimonial prospects depend on their capacity to handle work. Again, whether children like it or not, they have to work and earn money for meeting family requirements and for girls they are also specially prepared for meeting dowry requirements for marriage. The table above depicts that majority of children were not interested/liking with/in their job/work because of the reasons they put forward.

Wages

Children work on uncertain terms without fixed agreements. As a matter of fact many of them do not know how much they earn on an average. This may be due to the fact that salary depends as much as hours of work. However, they are aware of the fact that they are paid less than adults that do the same work. For many children salaries do not satisfy their daily needs.

Children's work provides better income to the families involved in the study area. It is seen that income derived from handcrafts and transport work was predominant when compared to the other sources. The hidden dimension relating to income, earning is children's active contribution. Following table 6.10 provides the statistical information of wages/income and receiving of wages.

It is inferred from the analysis that child workers are engaged in works with the ultimate aim of supplementing income at the cost of their childhood privileges. It is understood from the discussion that parents used to motivate their children to work more by making promises of providing modern dresses, shoes, ornaments and other things. Children are lured by the words of parents and constantly

Table 6.9: Distribution of Child Workers according to their Interest towards their Work and Reasons for Liking and Disliking the Work

S. No.	Liking				Frequency	Percentage
1.	Like				62	31.0
2.	Dislike				138	69.0
	Total				200	100
	Reasons for Liking	*No.*	*Percentage*	*Reasons for disliking*	*No.*	*Percentage*
1.	To earn money	143	71.5	Want to study	126	63.0
2.	Skill acquisition	74	37.0	No more interesting	87	43.5
3.	Interesting	59	29.5	See no future	109	54.5
4.	No other option	64	32.0	Parental force	142	71.0
5.	For parental satisfaction	78	39.0	Work is hazardous	64	32.0
6.				Underpaid	96	47.0
7.				Feel boring and monotonous	69	34.5
8.				Allows no time	43	21.5
9.				Affects recreation, playing and education	51	25.5

Source: Field study 2009.

Table 6.10: Distribution of Child Workers according to Wages/Income and Receiving of Wages

S. No.	Per Month Earning	No.	Percentage	Receiving of Salary	No.	Percen-tage
1.	Upto 500	63	31.5	Self	93	46.5
2.	501 to 1000	56	28.0	Parents	84	42.0
3.	1001 to 1500	38	19.0	Other relatives	23	11.5
4.	1501 to 2000	23	11.5			
5.	Above 2000	20	10.0			
	Total	200	100.0		200	100.0

Source: Field Study 2009.

engage themselves in different sectors of economy. Parents also fix up target and force the children accordingly to fulfill the same in view of maximizing their income. This is one of the reasons why children spent more time in work. Thus children are the potential source of income providers. This is precisely the reason why children are increasingly inducted in various works by violating their genuine rights.

A comprehensive attempt to study the income contribution made by child workers to their respective family indicated that they extended considerable amount of support to parents in terms of income derived through their work by meeting basic and necessary requirements of life at home. Therefore, it is clearly established in this study that they are the base in the families economically insecure at the family level in the study area. These children are put to work under a hostile atmosphere leaving their education and recreation, which are essential for childhood development. It is understood from the study that inspite of loosing hard earned money in the process of exploitation; children are able to make a good income as majority (57%) of them accepted that their monetary contribution improved their family life. The present study also divulges that about 60 per cent of the child workers were contributing in the ratio of 70:30 i.e. they were keeping 30 per cent of their earning with them and were giving 70 per cent to their families. Here one thing which was very strange was that though most of them were runaways, they were contributing to their families. However, there were also those who were not contributing even a single penny to their families. Another set of child workers opined that they do not provide money on a monthly basis. They used to save some amount every month and after saving a handsome amount, say somewhere between Rs. 2000 to 5,000, they provide that amount to their parents/ families. Yet another set of working children used to contribute to their families only on special occasions for example, wedding in the family, when someone fell ill or on festive occasions. One strange case we found was that of a young boy who was contributing to his family in a very unique way i.e. some amount to his parents, some for himself and some to his grand parents. Finally, there were some children who keep a very small amount with them and handover the rest of the amount to their parents. The children who were spending their wages on themselves varies as some were spending 50 per cent of the earning, some 90 per cent, some only 23 per cent and the rest between 15 to 60 per cent. They used to spend their income on dressing, smoking, and movies and even on food.

Loan Locations

In the field of indebtness, the study found that 39 per cent of the sampled child labourers were indebted. Indebtness was reported due to availing of loans for performing family functions, repaying old debts, meeting medical expenditure, arranging wedding ceremonies, etc. It is learnt from the discussion that people who are running finance business in the towns visit the villages wherever handicrafts and other related work is pursued in order to extend loans to local families and collect the same with weekly/monthly/yearly interest periodically. Amount of loan extended depended upon the number of children involved in work in family because it provides guarantee to the financier to collect the amount lent already without any constraints. Thus the families and their children made concerted efforts to have carpets, shawls etc. as much as possible in order to get rid of debt. This is the vicious cycle, which operates in the valley of Kashmir. Following Table 6.11 presents the details in the statistical form.

Working Conditions

So far as the working condition is concerned around half of the respondents (47%) said that it was alright and were satisfied with the working conditions but there were certain things which were lacking

Table 6.11: Classification of Respondents according to Loan and Repayment of Loan

S. No.	Loan locations	No.	Percentage	Repayment of loan	No.	Percentage
1.	Yes	78	39.0	Deduction from wages	88	44.0
2.	No	122	61.0	Doing extra work	62	31.0
3.				Parents repay yourself	38	19.0
4.				In other ways	12	6.0
	Total	200	100.0		200	100.0

Source: Field Study 2009.

at the workplace. Some said there were no toilet facility, some complained about drinking water, others said, they have to work in open space, etc. Sometimes the child workers were abused, sometimes beaten up and sometimes even their salaries were cut. Some of the sampled respondents (22%) said that the working conditions were good and only 13 and 15 per cent of respondents responded that working conditions were sad and harsh respectively. On the whole, leaving aside the above problems, the data reveals that the working conditions were normal.

Health Conditions

The available literature in general and review of related studies in particular provides ample evidence regarding the health risks to which child workers are exposed. This is precisely the reason why a separate-sub section on the issue of recreation and health is incorporated in the framework of analysis. This section studies the sources of recreation available to child workers and health problems faced by them. An important aspect dealt with here is the amount of energy spent by children in their work.

The important sources of recreation generally available to rural based children were identified and accordingly their opinion was elicited in relation to three major levels of frequency. How often these children are able to get recreation is the main focus against each source of recreation. Accordingly it is noted in Table 6.12. It was interesting to observe from the field that both male and female children view television with compromising either quality or efficiency.

Table 6.12: Distribution of Working Children According to Recreation Avenues available to Them and its Frequency

S. No.	Recreation Sources	Number of Children							
		QU		ST		NEV		Total	
		No.	Percentage	No.	Percentage	No.	Percentage	No.	Percentage
1.	Viewing Television	153	76.5	32	16.0	15	7.5	200	100.0
2.	Listening to radio	109	54.5	76	38.0	15	7.5	200	100.0
3.	Visiting friends and relatives	96	48.0	87	43.5	17	8.5	200	100.0
4.	Play	132	66.0	55	27.5	13	6.5	200	100.0

Note: QU: Quite often, ST: Sometimes, NEV: Never.

It is very interesting to observe from the field that whenever children go to the market and other places/areas for various reasons they get company of peer/friends. Sometimes these children join together in a common place in a particular house, which is spacious or under the tree and enjoy friendship. Apart these, there is a limited scope for mixing with friends. This a pathetic situation noted among child labourers. It is disheartening to note than an overwhelming majority of child workers (57.6%) never played any game due to their preoccupation with work.

It is inferred from the overall analysis that recreation, which is an important dimension of child development, is not made available to these children due to their total involvement in various forms of work. Practically these children never find time to recreate themselves and parents have also not realized the need for providing such facilities. Therefore, this situation, which is created by the existing culture, would impinge upon the balanced personality development of these children in future. Only single most recreation available to these children is television and viewing of it is combined with their regular work.

It is noted from table 6.13 that child workers have frequent headache and eye irritation due to their constant exposure to heavy work. Another important problem faced by child workers is joint pain. It is a well known fact that children spend more time on work, and performing such tasks requires continuous sitting by folding legs in the same posture. This produces joint pain in particular and

Table 6.13: Distribution of Child Labourers according to Predominant Health Problems specifically faced by Them

S. No.	*Health Problems*	*No. of Respondents*	*Percentage*
1.	Back pain	64	32.00
2.	Joint pain	85	42.5
3.	Respiratory problem	51	25.5
4.	Pain/Ache	83	41.5
5.	Stress/strain	44	22.0
6.	Headache/eye irritation	93	46.5
7.	No problem	81	40.5

Source: field study 2009.

body pain in general; yet another crucial problem faced by children is lack of appetite. These are crucial problems emerging from the hectic work, which impinges upon the overall health of tender aged children. About 40 per cent of children reported that they did not face any problem so far. It is learnt from the analysis that those children who have not faced any health trouble are new entrants to the field.

Many occupations are not hazardous by themselves but bad environment and working conditions makes them such. The various environmental factors such as ventilation, dust, gases, fumes, odors, lighting, noise, humidity, over-crowding, etc. threatens the child's health. Since children are still in the process of growing and attaining full physical stature, their growth is likely to be affected.

Any occupation which allows the working children to come in contact with harmful substances like chemicals, carpet industry, handicrafts industry, transport workshops, etc. is termed as intrinsically hazardous. Thus the implication on child labour can not be overstated. There is impairment of both physical and psychological health of children at a critical state of life often permanent consequences. But even more destructive to long term quality of life is the permanent damage to the social development. Lack of education condemns children to the worst employment prospects.

Effects of Child Labour on Psychological and Physical Health: A growth spurt in children starts in case of girls around 10 years and in boys around 12 years of age and continues till 16 years in girls and 17 years in boys. This growth spurt is delayed in case of malnourished children and in those who belong to poor families. Extra intake of calories and protein are essential in this stage to recuperate form malnutrition and to cover the puberty spurt. Moreover the working children need additional energy for their physical work.

The present study reveals that child labourers had always lower growth status on each nutritional group as compared to their nonworking counterpart (students). It has also been observed that children who started working early in life suffered from deterioration in their nutritional status but such impact was not seen for those children who started working after the age of 12 years.

Health effects of labour on children also vary according to the type of work situation. Children who are engaged in their own household jobs or family based industries have no direct adverse health effects. On the other hand bonded and wage child worker have greater impact on their health because of exploitative and unregulated nature of work where children are exposed more to physical and mental abuse. Most of the poor child workers go to work without adequate food, clothing and proper shelter. The obvious result of lending such a deprived life hampers the process of their normal growth and development.

Child labourers lack the basic psychological and emotional requirements such as love, security, development, independence and the opportunity to develop their personalities. Certainly, these working children are a product of persisting economic deprivation and insecurity. However, lack of awareness on issues relating to pollution and health and non implementation of the precision of law due to weak enforcement, have also contributed to the rising problem of child labour and their economic exploitation, as well as to the issues of environmental pollution which further increase the vulnerability of child workers.

Space

So far as the space for work is concerned, the sectors where work is performed inside/indoor, the space for work was more or less sufficient and satisfactory as majority of the sampled respondents responded positively. These sectors of work mostly include carpet weaving, *shawl bawfi, kaline bawfi*, and other handicrafts work, etc. So far as child workers in transport work, shops, hotels and restaurants, streets, were concerned, they were falling short of spaces as these kinds of units/ centers were mostly operating in the urban sectors of the valley where space/land, both for work (commercial) and other purposes is too expensive to have it.

Lunch and Tea Facilities

The table (6.14) shows statistically the detailed response of the child workers regarding the availability of lunch and tea facilities at the working units/centers.

Table 6:14: Classification of Respondents according to Facilities of Lunch and Tea at Working Places

S. No.	At Centre/ Unit	No.	Percentage	At Home	No.	Percentage
1.	Morning tea	—	—	Morning tea	189	94.5
2.	Lunch	117	58.5	Lunch	83	41.5
3.	Evening tea	104	52	Evening tea	159	79.5

Source: Field study 2009.

Holidays

Holidays are a must in order to relax and refresh oneself. Whether it is a child or an elderly person, every one needs the weekly holidays. In this back ground, the present study collected information about weekly and monthly holidays the child workers are getting. The following table (6.15) shows whether the working children were getting weekly and monthly holidays or not.

The children who were getting one/two off days in a week was in the sagacity that the markets including their centres/units of work remain closed on a particular day once a week mostly on Sundays, Fridays and sometimes on Saturdays. Hence the workers were not required on a particular day and in this way they got one day off. In case of domestic help, the children were mostly not enjoying weekly holidays, but most of them opined that during couple of days in a

Table 6.15: Classification of Child Labourers on Getting Weekly and Monthly Holidays

S. No.	Off-days in a Week	No.	Percentage	Off-days in a Month	No.	Percentage
1.	One	153	76.5	Five	143	71.5
2.	Two	44	22.0	Six	36	18.0
3.	Three	19	9.5	Seven	15	7.5
				Eight	17	8.5

Source: Field Study 2009.

week, they get six or seven hours break. During this break, they used to visit relatives, friends, or even to play cricket or some other game or used to watch television. In case of the self employed workers, they had no holiday routine as such. But whenever they felt like, they did not go out for work. However, their only motive was to earn more and more and as such they avoided any kind of holiday. On the whole, we can say that whether these were the self-employed workers or other workers, they were getting weekly holidays. However, there were some exceptions. Some of the child workers informed that during off-days they were going for agricultural work at home and some are going for cattle and sheep rearing.

Overtime Work

In order to earn more money, the working children sometimes do overtime work. Keeping this fact in mind, we asked them whether they were getting paid for overtime work. The data reveals that 145 (72.5%) children were getting paid for overtime work and the rest 55 (27.5%) were not getting overtime work paid. Some of the sampled child labourers were not going for overtime work. In some centres/ units children were having freedom for going for overtime work and earn extra money.

Example

A 14 year old boy from Qazigund, Anantnag declares: "I feel; that I am being misused. I work for a long time. This is not fair. The money they give me is not sufficient for my overtime work on the one hand, and on the other, the elders are paid more than me. The employer should give me uniform for the work, because my cloths get ruined. My wages are not sufficient to enable me to support my family, pay school fees for my siblings and buy new cloths. If my parents were in a good position financially, I would not have been working this time."

A good number (69%) of sampled respondents had to work even when they are not feeling well, whereas others (31%) are not going for any work during ill health. Around 53 per cent of sampled respondents responded that there is protection against work hazards whereas 47 per cent said there is no protection against work hazards. This all depends the type of work child is involved with as some sectors are hazardous like transport workshops, handicrafts and some are not like domestic work, and work in hotels and restaurants.

Rest Intervals

After knowing the details about overtime work, we asked them about the hours they spent as rest interval or whether they are having any rest interval other than lunch break. Majority (53%) of the respondents responded that there was no rest interval other than lunch break. It was disheartening to note that such a huge number of children said that they were not getting any rest interval during the course of the day. Only 43 per cent working children replied that they were getting a kind of rest interval. These children were mostly those who were working in handicraft centers' or work as domestic labourers. After the rush hour (lunch time), the worker get half an hour or so to relax. After relaxing, they again went to work as it was time for serving evening tea and sneaks. Another revealing fact was that majority (62%) of children were getting leave with pay. They were mostly working in the centres of carpet weaving, shawl bawfi and other handicrafts work. These children also brought it to our notice that reasons for being on leave were investigated by the employers. Mostly during illness/sick and other unavoiding reasons leave is being sanctioned. Around 38 per cent of sampled respondents were not being paid for leave. Mostly sectors of transport workshops, hotels and restaurants, etc. were not paying any kind of remuneration for leave.

Children's Behaviour about Nature of Work and Satisfaction with the Behaviour of Employer

Generally, children are employed as helpers to do all kinds of odd jobs related or unrelated to employers business. Only a small number of children are taken as learners and given independent job assignment in due course of time, but in some vocations, the nature of work is such that it does not require any skill. Here the children start working and earning from the beginning. There are a few jobs which require skills. The skill for doing the job can be learnt according to the nature of work. Sometimes, it takes a few years for a person to become skilled craftsman. There are a few jobs, which do not require any training and skills, e.g. domestic service, tea shop and restaurant work, shop attendant, etc. In this context child workers were asked about the satisfaction with the behaviour of the employer. More or less almost all the child labourers were satisfied with their employers. We also asked the child labourers about their likes and dislikes for the present job. They gave different and multiple reasons. These include economic gains, skill and career development, extraneous reasons. Within the economic gains reason include; getting money, helping family financially, easy income, no investment, getting maximum earnings which no other occupation can give, managing pocket expanses, food, saving for future and dowry and helping in repayment of family debts. Skill and career development covers reasons like getting training in new skills, for better future prospects like becoming foreman or establishing business/work shop when they grow up. Extraneous reasons include simple job, family occupation, not risky and non-hazardous, benefit of working at home, no binding of time, full security to girls, no risk, near to residence.

When asked about the reasons for not liking the job; work in open, no shelter, long hours of work, low wages, bad working conditions, exploitation by employers, abuses, physical violence, unhealthy, dingy, congested, dirty environment, work out of desperation, deduction in the wages, etc. Table 6.16 indicates the reasons for liking/disliking the present job.

Table 6.16: Child Workers Opinion Indicating Reasons for Liking and Disliking the Jobs by Sex

Sex	No Response	Reasons for Liking			Reasons for not Liking			Total
		Economic Benefits	Skill and Career Development	Extraneous Reasons	Tiresome/ Risky/ Hazardous	Out of Desperatio n	Other Reasons	
Boys	10 55.55	29.5 50.86	14 36.36	9.5 67.85	24 36.36	8.5 32.07	4.5 69.23	100.0 (138) 69.00
Girls	8 44.44	28.5 49.13	24.5 63.63	4.5 32.14	14.5 63.63	18 67.92	2 30.67	100.0 (62) 31.00
Total (f) Percentage	100 (18) 9.00	100 (58) 29.00	100 (38.5) 19.25	100 (14) 7.00	100 (38.5) 19.25	100 (26.5) 13.25	100 (6.5) 3.25	100.0 (200) 100.0

Source: Field Study 2009.
f = frequency

Reaction of Family Members about Economic Contribution

The reaction of family members about the economic contribution of the child workers is very important. If the children get a very good response and respect towards their economic contribution in the family, it results in the positive influence on the behaviour of the child, which sometimes leads to undue exploitation of the child. It has been observed in the field that in both cases children are getting exploited i.e. whether getting positive or negative response. The following Table (6.17) shows it in detail.

Table 6.17: Distribution of Child Labourers on the Reaction of Family Members about their Economic Contribution

S. No.	*Reaction of Family Members*	*No.*	*Percentage*	*Allowing Visitors at Workplace of Child Labourers*	*No.*	*Percentage*
1.	Happy	113	56.5	Yes	137	68.5
2.	Sad	41	20.5	No	67	31.5
3.	Angry	42	21.0			

Source: Field Study 2009.

When asked about the visit of relatives to their workplace, majority (69%) of the sampled child labourers responded positively.

Number of Employees Working at the Work Place

We also enquired from the child labourers about the number of children/employees working at the place of work/unit/centre. Majority (53 %) of the respondents bring it to our notice that less then ten child labourers are working in their centres/units. This was mostly found in the handicraft centres and other carpet weaving centres and also in agricultural activities, 35 per cent of the sampled respondents disclosed that 11 to 20 child labourers are working in their units/ centres. These children were working at different locations in various centres including handicrafts, transport workshops, hotels and restaurants, etc. owned by different individuals in partnership. It was observed that due to legal and other hindrances, children were put to work at different locations. The following Table 6.18 provides a detailed picture.

Table 6.18: Number of Children/Employees Working at the Workplace

S. No.	Number of Children/Employees at the Working Place	Number	Percentage
1.	1 to 10	105	52.5
2.	11 to 20	70	35.0
3.	21 to 30	21	10.5
4.	31 and above	4	2.0
	Total	200	100.0

Source: Field Study 2009.

Child Labour Laws

A spacious vision of the Constitution of India brings within its conspectus almost everything the Convention on the Rights of the Child (CRC) adopted by the United Nations and ratified by majority of countries including India, has spelt out. We are in 2009 but the intervening decade has suffered from legislative amnesia; although every ratifying country is under an international obligation to implement the principles and provisions of the CRC. No comprehensive enactment on the lines of the CRC has come into being so far. One major change the CRC has stressed is the switch from the basic needs approach to the proactive fundamental rights approach. This study also flows from the (Indian) Constitutional mandates in parts 3rd and 4th. It is perfectly open to the Central Government to legislate on child rights because the treaty-making power confers law making authority on the Union (Article 253). The National Commission for Children (has it become law yet?) bill is a partial actualization of the CRC obligation.

While legislation has lagged behind, the Supreme Court has adopted an activist, creative and dynamic role, which has opened up an expensive legal regime in the matter of child welfare. It was in the above mentioned context that we asked the child labourers about the knowledge of laws and their existence and application in Kashmir. The following table shows it in detail.

Table 6.19: Classification of Child Labourers according to the Knowledge of Laws and Their Application

S. No.	Knowledge about Laws	No.	Percentage	Exist/Applied	No.	Percentage
1.	Yes	39	19.5	Yes	15	38.46
(a)	Minimum Age	31	79.48	No	5	12.82
(b)	Minimum Wage	2	5.12	Don't know	19	48.77
(c)	Hazardous Work	3	7.69			
(d)	Working Conditions	1	2.56			
(e)	All of the above	4	10.25			
2.	No	161	80.5			
	Total	200	100.00		39	100.0

Source: Field Study 2009.

There still exists in different parts of the valley, a system of usury, which the debtor or his descendents or dependents have to work for the creditor without reasonable wages or with no wages in order to extinguish the debt. The system implies the infringement of the basic human right and destruction of the dignity of human labour. These innocent souls remain unaware about the legal dimensions of this menace due to the discrimination and exploitation they are facing through red hands people. The table 6.19 depicts the knowledge and application of legal and constitutional measures in children under work.

When asked about the abolition of child labour, majority (67 per cent) of them responded in the favour of its abolition whereas 33 per cent said that they are not in favour of its abolition as it will affect them seriously. It was also observed in the field that its total abolition will result in more serious consequences. If child labour is eliminated, around half (50 per cent) will feel good whereas 18 and 32 per cent will feel sad and indifferent respectively.

Other Working Child/Children in the Family

Our next query to the child workers was regarding the other working child/children in their families. This was felt important so as to understand the family character and prevailing labour episode of the families of working children. About 37 per cent working children are having other children working whereas 53 per cent are not having any other child working in their families. About 47 per cent of child labourers are being punished for not doing domestic work and 53 per cent of child labourers are not humiliated or punished.

Satisfaction with Present Life Circumstances

After knowing and discussing the viewpoint of child workers regarding various components of job situation, one would naturally like to know the level of overall satisfaction of child workers with the work they are engaged in. The responses of child workers are presented in Table 6.20.

Table 6.20: Child Labourers Indicating whether They are Satisfied with Their Present Job/Life Circumstances

S. No.	*Dissatisfied*	*Indifferent*	*Satisfied*	*Total Percentage*	*Sex*
1.	45 (34.61)	23 (17.69)	62 (47.69)	130 (100.0)	Boys
2.	31 (44.28)	15 (21.42)	24 (34.28)	70 (100.0)	Girls
Total frequency percentage	76 (38.0)	38 (19.0)	86 (43.0)	200 (100.0)	

Source: Field Study 2009.

Table 6.20 indicates that nearly a little less than half are satisfied, 19 per cent did not provide any opinion and the remaining were dissatisfied with their present life circumstances.

Foreseeing Future

Our last and final query to them was regarding their future plan as every human being has a desire for the future life. Table 6.21 shows the future plan desire of the child workers.

The table 6.21 reveals that majority of working children (77 per cent) like to be very rich person and for that purpose they expressed their desire to join some other work. This is a clear indication of informal sector workers as generally, people working in informal sectors do not stay in a particular job for a long time. Similarly, the working children of Kashmir valley also like to change their job from time to time on various grounds. On the other hand 36 and 26 per cent of them see their future bright and promising respectively.

Table 6.21: Classification of Child Workers according to their Future Desire/Plan

S. No.	*Foreseeing Future*	*No.*	*Percentage*	*Like to be in Future*	*No.*	*Percentage*
1.	Bright	72	36.0	Rich Person	153	76.5
2.	Promising	52	26.0	Doctor/engineer	56	27.0
3.	Not bad	42	21.0	Govt. job	48	24.0
4.	Can't say	44	22.0	Private job	17	8.5
5.				Job abroad	35	17.5
6.				Educated	23	11.5
7.				Businessman	32	16.5

Source: Field Study 2009.

Child Labour and Human Rights

UNICEF estimates that out of the total number of children out of school, 54 per cent of them are girls. Many of these children work but traditional indicators of child labour often underestimate the amount of girls work because they ignore household chores. The human rights principle of non-discrimination requires that all work by children-whether of a domestic nature or not-be considered equally in the analysis of child labour.

As early as 1921, when the International Labour Organization (ILO) passed the first Minimum Age Convention, the world has attempted to protect children's right to an education and to prevent any child labour which would prejudice their school attendance. The ILOs Minimum Age Convention 138 of 1973 set the standard for the minimum age for admission to employment as 15 years, or in special cases where educational and economic facilities are insufficiently developed, 14 years; light work not harmful to the child or prejudicial to his or her attendance at school is permissible after age 12. Since 1990, with the entry into force of the Convention on the Rights of the Child, the child's right to be protected from "an work that is likely to be hazardous or to interfere with the child's education" and his or her right, on an equal, nondiscriminatory basis to 'primary education compulsory and available free to all" have gained the status of internationally recognized norms' while imposing an obligation on the 192 states parties to the Convention to realize these rights for the children under their jurisdiction. In

2000, children were provided further protection through the entry into force ILO Convention 182, which was ratified by 150 countries as of May 2004. Convention 182 prohibits the worst forms of child labour, defined as all forms of slavery and similar practices; child prostitution and pornography; illicit activities (in particular the production and trafficking of drugs); and work that is likely to harm the health, safety or morals of children.

The process of globalization has resulted in domination of market-oriented economy, where the state has become weak and the government and the electorate representatives have lost control over a number of things. In this context the ' Rights of the Child' is significant and important, because among the founding principles of that institution, to the world community still stands committed to, is of course the charter of Human Rights. The charter of Human Rights and the literature on rights has grown over the years. Its role is still a bit marginal but, nonetheless, in the context of globalization, a number of demands, which used to be made to states, not so much a matter of right but as a matter of development and the distribution of development, are now being demanded from the world community in the language of the international governments on human rights.

The human rights literature, as it has developed in the United Nations, has really two parts to it. The first part, the governance of civil rights, civil and political rights is something to which everybody agrees and everybody signed it. Of course a lot of countries do not do it. But there is another set of human rights; the economic, social and cultural rights, which constitute together with the civil and political rights. The major substance of human right discourse the world over is now economic, social and cultural right. However, some of the countries, including USA, have still not signed this important charter of Rights. But apart from the USA, the economic, social and cultural rights are more or less accepted by most members of the United Nations. It, therefore, demands certain norms of economic, social and cultural rights not only from certain individual member states but also from the whole world community. Among these social, cultural and political rights, there is no such thing as child rights. Child rights are mentioned, but in civil and political rights. There are rights against abuse of various kinds but they are not the part of the economic, social and cultural rights.

But at the same time the economic, social and cultural rights, as defined by the governments, have been limited to four areas, which are of vital importance to children. These areas are health, education, work and food. The right to food, the right to education, the right to work and the right to health, they are, of course, at different stages of agreement. But it is in that context that the word 'Right' of children needs to be linked with these four areas, which have been more or less glorified in international legal terminology.

In the present study when we asked the child labourers about their parental perception in the context of considering education as time consuming, money consuming and unproductive exercise for their children, majority (82.5 per cent) of the respondents shook their heads to convey yes that education is being considered the same, whereas 17.5 per cent said no. According to them it is the economic condition of the family which forces them to be in work rather then parental perception considering education as time, money consuming and unproductive work. We also enquired from the child labourers about the force their parents use for putting them to work due to their indebtness to the employer/owner and majority responded against whereas 37 per cent said that they are forced by their parents to go for work and release them from indebtness.

Application of human rights principles has led UNICEF into actions which identify, advocate for, and support communities of ethnic and racial groups suffering from discrimination, and to seek gender equity in all its actions. This means that the gender dimension of child labour has to be visible, a prelude to being understood and acted upon. The present study discovered and observed it in the field that girl children are being discriminated in terms of premature and exploitative forms of work, including more work and low wages as 63 per cent respondents' responded positive and 37 per cent negatively. The following table (6.22) shows the gender discrimination and their reasons for it.

Table 6.22: Classification of Child Labourers Indicating whether Girl Children are Discriminated in terms of Premature and Exploitative Forms of Work

S. No.	*Discrimi-nation*	*No.*	*Percen-tage*	*Reasons*	*No.*	*Percen-tage*
1.	Yes	127	63.5	Low wages than boys	76	38.00
2.	No	73	36.5	Less facilities than boys	63	31.5
3.				More work than boys	57	28.5
4.				Discrimination against other facilities	84	42.00
	Total	200	100.00			

Source: Field Study 2009.

In the present study, we also asked the child labourers about the people responsible for challenging their right to education and happy childhood without a work load etc. Majority (58.5 per cent) of the child workers blamed their parents, 27 per cent their brothers and sisters, 8 per cent government, 13 per cent employers/owners whereas 34 per cent of child labourers put this responsibility on their other relatives for stopping them to enjoy the childhood and educational life as young souls.

Knowledge of Children's Rights

A number of important observations were made also in the present study at the same time when collecting the data. It was observed in the field that people are unaware about the children's rights. It was in this context that we asked the child labourers about the knowledge of children's rights. Majority (69.5 per cent) of the child labourers were having some kind of knowledge and awareness about children's rights including right to education (78 per cent), right to childhood and free from work (46.5 per cent). Thirty nine per cent were not having any knowledge about children's rights.

Children not only have rights to health, nutrition and education, they have rights to protection, freedom from violence and exploitation, and to "a safe and supportive environment". The seventh major goal of the World Summit for Children called for the protection of children in especially difficult circumstances, particularly in situations of conflict. According to the plan of action, children in especially difficult circumstances included orphans and street children, refugee or displaced children, child workers, children trapped in prostitution or sexual abuse, disabled children and delinquent children. In decade since, a much clearer understanding has developed of the issues central to protecting children and guaranteeing their civil rights.

In the present study we also asked to the child labourers about the knowledge that children are not allowed to work in harsh and frightening circumstances. Most (58 per cent) of the child labourers were not knowing anything about it and only 42 per cent of child labourers were having some kind of knowledge about working in harsh and bad working conditions. At the same time we enquired from children about Human Rights violations in case of children through parents and employers, the understanding and knowledge under Human Rights Conventions and other legislations, they are having which is punishable. Only seven per cent children knew about it whereas 93 per cent did not know anything about it. The children were cherishing to ensure social, political and economic lives to children which are in a great way in the interest of human rights in the contemporary setting.

About 66.5 per cent children were aware about the existence and perpetuation of child labour as one of the main limiting factors in the way of human development of the family, individual and community whereas 33.5 per cent responded otherwise. Children's rights are the perceived human rights of children with particular attention to the rights of special protection and care afforded to the young, including their right to association with both biological parents, human identity as well as the basic needs for food, universal state-paid education, health care and criminal laws appropriate for the age and development of the child. Interpretation of children's rights range from allowing children the capacity for autonomous action to the enforcement of children being physically, mentally and emotionally free from abuse, exploitation and oppression. It was in this context that we asked the child workers about the awareness of UN Convention on the Rights of the Child to education, self expression and freedom from exploitative work, and about 98 per cent children did not know anything about it whereas only about 2 per cent were having some kind of understanding about the same.

Scholarly study generally focuses children's rights by identifying rights. The following rights allow children grow up healthy and free:

1. Freedom of speech,
2. Freedom of thought,
3. Freedom from fear,
4. Freedom of choice and the right to make decisions,
5. Ownership over one's body.

In a similar fashion, the Child Rights Information Network categorizes rights into two groups:

1. Economic, social and cultural rights, related to the conditions necessary to meet basic human needs such as food, shelter, education, health care, and gainful employment. Included are rights to education, adequate housing, food, water, the highest standard of health, the right to work and rights at work, as well as the cultural rights of minorities and indigenous peoples.
2. Environmental, cultural and developmental rights, which are sometimes called "third generation rights", and including the right to live in safe and healthy environments and that groups of people have the right to cultural, political, and economic development.

Parents/Guardians and Employers Perception about Child Labour, its Conditions and Consequences

Apart from what the child workers have said about their employment conditions it is equally important and interesting to ascertain the opinion of their parents/guardians on this point in order to understand the problem in its right perspective. This section deals with the opinion of parents towards the child's education without disturbing work, wage conditions and working conditions and also opinion of parents on the abolition of child labour and areas of employment of children, etc.

In India around 30 per cent population is below poverty line. It persists in every state of the country, though its concentration is more in certain states and castes. Ideally, child labour is an anathema, outrageous to human conscience and dignity. Its abolition is advocated on moral and ethical grounds but the reality of the situation is otherwise. As long as poverty exists in all its nakedness, child labour is bound to exist in either open or disguised form. What ultimately would matter is not the sentiments of the elites and managers of society, but the perception of those who are directly involved as actors in the phenomenon of child labour. It would therefore, be expedient and useful in formulating realistic policies, if we could ascertain the views of parents, employers and child workers on various aspects of child labour.

What is the level of education, will be clear if we go through the statistics of literacy in our country. Even after various educational programmes like adult education, formal education, etc. only 65 per cent population is found to be literate. If parents perceive the importance of children's education they may think of some alternative ways to educate them. The parents were therefore, asked whether they considered education necessary for children. Similarly parents were asked all questions relating to child's work, health, wages, etc.

In the unorganized sector, the entrepreneurs prefer to employ children to maximize their profits, because they constitute a cheap, silent, uncomplaining work force. Even in the organized sector, the children are hardly ever paid the legal maximum wages. It is against this background that a detailed description of the employers' opinion regarding reasons and modes of employing children, working conditions of children, wage conditions, their views about abolition of child labour, etc. are being covered in the ensuing paragraphs.

The children are employed in various types of working units/ centres. The present chapter covers besides profile of employers, the size of establishment, furnishing of surety/security, punishment to children for committing mistakes and offences, methods and modes of payment of wages, holidays, leave facilities, physical facilities and other fringe benefits. Employer's views regarding child labour, which includes effects of abolition of child labour on the child, his/her/their family, poor families, on society in general, etc. are also discussed. Along with this, information regarding knowledge of the employers about various legislations—prohibiting and regulating child labour, difficulties faced and suggestions made by employers in the proper implementation of these acts are included in this section. A sample of thirty five employers has been taken.

Personal Information of the Parents/Guardians

In the personal information of the parents' number of questions were asked including age, sex, address, family size, educational level and occupation.

Age and Sex Composition

When parents/guardians were asked to indicate their age, there were different age groups of parents for which the table (6.23) below gives/ shows the data in detail.

Table 6.23: Classification of Parents/Guardians by the Age Group

S. No.	*Age Group*	*Number*	*Percentage*
1.	30-40 years	25	35.71
2.	40-50 years	35	50.00
3.	50-60 years	10	14.29
	Total	70	100.00

Source: Field Study 2009.

So the age of the parents/guardians of the child labourers ranging between 30 to 60 years which means both young and old parents were sending their children to work. So any specific age group of parents/guardian is not responsible for sending their children to work though it was more between 40 to 50 years of age. The data also shows it clearly that majority of the heads of the households 63 (90%) were males and only 7 (10 per cent) of the households of child labourers were headed by a female who were interviewed. Most heads of the households interviewed were from rural areas.

Family Size

The heads of the households were further asked about the size of their families. No doubt most of the families were joint as such the strength of the families also shows the characteristic of child labour. Following table shows the size of the family of the sampled households (table 6.24).

Table 6.24: Size of the Family according to Head of the Household of Child Labourers

S. No.	Size	Number	Percentage
1.	5-10 member	57	81.42
2.	10-15 members	13	18.57
	Total	70	100.00

Source: Field Study 2009.

The Table discloses that 57 (81.42%) households are having their family strength between 5 to 10 members whereas 13 (18.57%) were having it 10 to 15. Majority 48 (68.57%) heads of the households of working children were illiterate and only 22 (31.42%) were literate. This shows the weak educational level of families of child labourers.

Occupation

The next question which was asked to the head of the households was about their occupation. This shows whether the work of the child labourers' is hereditary or tradition of the family for them. The following table (6.25) shows the occupation of the heads of the households.

Table 6.25: Occupation of the Heads of the Households of the Child Labourers

S. No.	Occupation	Number	Percentage
1.	Daily labourer	32	45.71
2.	Govt. employer	9	12.57
3.	Farmer	25	35.71
4.	Contractor	4	5.71
	Total	70	100.00

Source: Field Study 2009.

The tables (6.25) above shown reveals that 32 (45.71%) respondents were daily labourers, 9 (12.57%) were govt. employees, 25 (35.71%) were farmers, 4 (5.71%) were contractors. This shows that child labourers of different family backgrounds were in the work market in Kashmir. So we can not say that children from a specific parental background were in work. No doubt insecure economic situation of the family can be the background for most of the children to be in work.

Number of Children Studying and Working in the Family

When a child is employed, certain problems arise. Economic necessity to support the family is justified under certain distressing circumstances. The child is deprived of play and education. This precludes him from taking part in most productive participation in the privileges and obligation of citizenship. Education is by and large the greatest input for the development of an individual adult or child. Education becomes a way of investing in human capital and hence individuals have to be equipped with capabilities necessary for modern societies. Besides other factors, the progress of education of children also depends upon the attitude of the parents towards education of their children. Literate parents influence their children in several ways in taking up education earnestly and illiteracy of parents acts as a cultural constraint on the progress of education among children. Many children who are in the process of acquiring knowledge are suddenly deprived of it when they are asked by their parents to go for wage labour or earn independently. These children from poor socio-economic stratum have to start work at very tender age and they have been deprived of all opportunities of growth and development. The head of the households were asked about the number of children of their family studying. Following table (6.26) shows it in detail.

Table 6.26: Number of Children Studying in the Family

S. No.	Response	Number	Percentage
1.	No	9	12.85
2.	One studying	22	31.42
3.	Two and above studying	39	55.71
	Total	65	100.00

Source: Field Study 2009.

About 54 (77.14%) heads of the household said that they are having only one working child in the family. And 16 (22.85%) responded that they are having either two or more than two working children in the family. The data also delineates that 19 (27.14%) heads of the households have their children in work from last one year whereas 38 (54.28%) said that their children are in work from last two years and 13 (18.57%) heads of the households responded that their children are in work from last three years. About 62 (88.57%) heads of the households responded that their working children fall under the age group of 11 to 14 years whereas only 8 (11.42%) responded that their children, were falling under the 8—11 years age group.

The Work in which Children are Engaged

The reactions of the heads of the households were about the work in which their children engaged are presented in the table 6.27.

Table 6.27: Classification of Children according to Work by the Heads of Households

S. No.	Work Engaged	Number	Percentage
1.	Shawl Bwafi	29	41.42
2.	Embroidery	23	32.85
3.	Knitting*	11	15.71
4.	Carpet weaving	39	55.71
5.	Hotel and restaurant	23	32.85
6.	Agriculture	31	44.28
7.	Domestic work	35	50.00
8.	Street work	21	30.00

* knitting includes sweaters, socks, caps, etc. making.

Table 6.27 shows that carpet weaving (55.71%), agriculture (44.28%), shawl bwafi (41.42%), etc. are the dominant sectors in Kashmir where innocent young souls are put to work for narrow and short gains by their parents. These are infact the hidden sectors where children are working more in number as they are confined to household business.

Nature of Work

The nature of work means whether the child labour is a daily, temporary or a monthly based worker. The following table (6.28) shows it in detail.

Table 6.28: Nature of Work of the Child Labourers according to Their Parents

S. No.	*Nature of work*	*Number*	*Percentage*
1.	Daily worker	27	38.57
2.	Temporary worker	9	12.85
3.	Monthly worker	34	48.57
	Total	70	100.00

Source: Field Study 2009.

Table 6.28 reveals that 27 (38.57%) parents have their children as daily workers, 9 (12.85%) as temporary workers whereas 34 (48.57%) have their children as monthly workers.

Reason for Sending Children to Work

It is generally economic hardship and some time socio-cultural factors which compel parents/guardians to give more importance to work than education. The samples heads of the household put varied reasons for sending child/children to work. The following table (6.29) shows it in detail.

Table 6.29: Reason for Sending Child/Children to Work according to their Parents

S. No.	*Reasons*	*Number*	*Percentage*
1.	Lack of quality education	23	32.85
2.	Inaccessibility of schools	11	15.71
3.	Cultural role/tradition	17	24.28
4.	Skill acquisition	33	47.14
5.	Poverty	36	51.42

Source: Field Study 2009.

Table (6.29) shows that there are number of reasons responsible for sending children to work according to their parents. Not a single cause is responsible for child labour as 23 (32.85%) parents blame lack of quality education responsible for sending their children to work, inaccessibility of schools is also a factor adding to the magnitude of child labour, 17 (24.28%) said that it is because of cultural role/ tradition, 33 (47.14%) parents said being in work at an early age is necessary for skill acquisition for future life, whereas 36 (51.42%) parents responded that their children are in work only because of poor economic condition at home.

The reasons for employing children for employers can be manifold. The view points of the parents/guardians were presented in the above paragraph. When employers were asked on this point, they gave variety of responses as shown in table 6.30.

Table 6.30: Employers Indicating Reasons for Employing Children

S. No.	Reasons	Number	Percentage
1.	Skill acquisition	31	88.57
2.	Low payment	20	57.14
3.	Helping poverty stricken families	29	82.85
4.	Long hours work	13	37.14
5.	For having soft fingers and hands	22	62.85
6.	Only option	15	33.33

Source: Field Study 2009.

Contribution of Children to Family Income

The contribution of children to family income is ultimately what forces them into work market. The following Table (6.31) shows the contribution children are making to their families on a monthly basis.

Table 6.31: Parental Opinion about the Contribution of Child Labourers to Family Income

S. No.	Contribution	Number	Percentage
1.	Below Rs. 500/-	13	18.57
2.	Rs. 500 to Rs 1000/-	19	27.14
3.	Rs. 1000 to Rs. 2000	22	31.42
4.	Above Rs. 2000	16	22.85
	Total	70	100.00

Source: Field Study 2009.

Table 6.31 reveals that 13 (18.57%) children contribute below Rs. 500 per month to family income, 19 (27.14%) contribute between Rs. 500 to Rs. 1000, 22 (31.42%) contribute between Rs. 1000 to Rs. 2000 whereas 16 (22.85%) parents responded that their children contribute more than Rs. 2000 per month to family income. Most of the child labourers receive their salary by themselves as responded by their parents.

Facilities at the Working Centre/Unit

The question of the availability of basic necessary facilities in the working centre/unit to the child labourers has got the crucial importance. It is because the availability of basic facilities affects the health of child labourers. Many sociological and other studies have revealed that the continued child labour has certainly affected adversely in the absence of or insufficient availability of minimum human facilities. The general impression too is that neither all basic human facilities are provided to the child labourers in the working centres/units nor all children get these facilities at all times. In this regard, we made a default enquiry from the children, their employers and their parents. In response, the parents mentioned the following facilities available in their working units/ centres (table 6.32).

Table 6.32: Facilities Available to Child Labourers at the Working Units/Centres

S. No.	*Facilities Provided*	*Number*	*Percentage*
1.	Toilet/urinal	18	25.71
2.	Electricity	9	12.85
3.	Water	63	90.00
4.	Entertainment	7	10.00
5.	Cleanliness	19	27.14
6.	Heating arrangement	23	32.85
7.	Good environment	14	20.00

Source: Field Study 2009.

The data presented in the above table (6.32) need the sociological explanation/analysis which follows.

The cumulative response regarding the necessary facilities provided to the child labourers at their places of work by the parents are very crucial without which no work can be carried out. At the same time, this statistical response reveals the empirical conditions in reality. These facilities do not represent all or maximum facilities, but do reveal many facilities to the minimum extent. These facilities included toilet/urinal, electricity, water, entertainment, cleanliness, heating arrangement and good environment, etc.

Regarding the heating arrangement as Kashmir remains very cold during winter (e.g. Dras-the recorded coldest region in the world with -45 Degree Celsius during winters), the crude fact is that heating arrangement is being provided during winters to the child labourers at the handicraft centres, etc. Our investigation revealed that, in actuality, much needed heating during the entire winter season is provided by the traditional bukharis (a local system of heating the room). This is how in winters work is carried inspite of severe winter and in this way cold is not allowed to become an impediment in work.

Satisfaction with Facilities

The investigations revealed that very less number of the parents 26 (37.14%) are satisfied with the available facilities to the child labourers at working units/centres. Most of the sampled respondents 44 (62.85%) are not satisfied with the facilities to their children.

Table 6.33: Reasons for no Satisfaction with the Facilities

S. No.	*Reasons for no Satisfaction*	*Number*	*Percentage*
1.	Availability of electricity	39	55.71
2.	Entertainment facility	24	34.28
3.	Toilet/urinal facility	41	58.57
4.	Modern equipments	31	44.28
5.	Ventilator	19	27.14

Source: Field Study 2009.

The majority of the sampled parents are not satisfied with the facilities due to lack of electricity, entertainment, toilet/urinal, modern equipment, ventilator, etc. to the child labourers. In actuality, the instruments which are used in the handicraft units/centres, etc. are old and child labourers have to work with the obsolete instruments. The entertainment at the working centres was considered necessary by all the groups of the respondent's including parents mainly because of the repetitive nature of the handicrafts work, domestic work, hotel and restaurant work, etc.

Wage Conditions

The most widespread feeling among the concerned people is that the wages for the handicraft items, domestic work, street work, etc. are solely determined by the employers who employ children for obvious reasons in their units/centres. It is partly because of historical reasons here and partly because of less attention by government towards these sectors of the economy. In this situation, the employers of the various units/centres take a lot of benefit and carry out the highest degree of exploitation on the child labourers. In response to our investigation, all the parent respondents gave the response that the wages for child labourers are exclusively determined by the owners of these centers'. However, while majority of the parents 57 (81.42%) interviewed mention the name of employers and 13 (18.57%) mention the name of government which determines wages of the work of the child labourers in some of the sectors including handicrafts according to them. It may be argued here that the employers emerge as the sole arbitral of the child labour wages and middleman and government have least role in it. Thus, the employers have the dominant and determining role of exploitation of the child labourers.

Criteria for Determining Wages

Another related query of the proceeding theme, our investigation was carried out in order to know about the procedure/criterion through which the wages for the work of child labourers are determined. The responses of parents reveal that there are not clear set rules/laws or directions/guidelines on the part employers or govt., for determination of wages of handicrafts work, etc. The employers take full advantage of the situation and dictate their terms on the child labourers in the field of wages and other matters. All this leads to the highest degree of exploitation of the child labourers. Since most of these units/centres in this part of the state in unorganized sector, the government does not feel any urgency to take stock of the present situation. Since a lot of exploitation of the child labourers is going on in the handicraft centres as well as in other sectors of the economy, the government was supposed to intervene to stop the exploitation of the child labourers. When an investigation was made about the government's role in this regard, the role was found quite apathetic. It hardly took any serious interest in this field.

Collection of Wages and Payment of Wages

In the related functional dynamics, it seems important that the employers pay Child labourers their wages in time and regularly. This keeps the health of the child labourers as well as the working unit/ centres normal. In order to know the real situation regarding the collection and regularity of the wages, we made a relevant enquiry and its response follows that while 26 (74.28%) employers conveyed that the child worker collects wages himself whereas 9 (25.71%) employers responded that the wages are collected by the parents of the child labourers. As far as the payment of wages is concerned most of the employers 23 (65.71%) informed that payment is made monthly whereas some employers conveyed that payment is also made weekly if the situation is such.

These responses of the employers are clearly opposite and hiding the reality. Taking into consideration various aspects of the problem, our feeling is that the child labourers are not paid regularly and also according to their labour which is a hard fact. Infact, the situation is pathetic and cruel especially in far flung villages of Kashmir. It was reported that in some cases the wages are paid after a huge gap and are not full but partial.

Fulfillment of Basic Needs at Home

Since the output of the working units/centres is huge, the wages of the child labourers should have been of the equal standard. But the situation is quite different. Despite the fact that the employers earn a lot of profit from the production of their units/centres, the child labourers are paid very less amount of wages. So, it is very difficult for them to satisfy the basic needs at home through this little amount.

Receiving an Advance Payment or Loan

It has commonly been observed throughout India that parents of the child labourers receive advance payment or loans from their employers for their own complex conditions. Though the problems of the child labourers for the time being get resolved, the long term implications prove disastrous to the child labourers as well as to the parents. It has specifically been observed that a good percentage of sampled parents 24 (34.28%) have received an advance payment or loan from the employers of the child labourers. The research discovered that the amount of loan is specifically used for the domestic needs like clothing, medicine, education of other children in the family, and so on. It was also observed that the advance payment or loan received from the employer is taken back in a way in which lot of exploitation and injustice is made to the child labourers and parents of the child labourers. In a situation in which no formal documentation takes place, the employers determine the wages as well as take back this amount on their own conditions and according to their own wishes. It may be mentioned here that the loan scenario benefits the employers at the cost of child labourers and their parents. The parents as well as the child labourers reported that once they take any loan of any amount from the employers it has its repercussions on the wages to repay the loan. Although there was a very little percentage of parents of child labourers who had taken loan but they were not in a position to highlight it as according to them it will affect them badly. All the parents were repaying the loan through children's wages and by extra work of the child.

Labour and Career

It is disheartening to note that 42 (60.00%) of parents considered labour necessary for shaping the carrier of a child. This shows the level of understanding about the importance of education in shaping and moulding ones behaviour and carrier. Whereas 28 (40.00%) of parents are against the belief that labour helps in shaping career of a child. We at the same time tried to find out the reasons why/how labour helps in shaping the career of a child.

The table (6.34) indicates that skill acquisition at an early age helps in shaping carrier of a child whereas some parents believe that earning money at so an early age is very fruitful for future role in life and is ready to take the role of a mature person.

Table 6.34: Opinion of Parents on How Labour Helps in Shaping Career of a Child

S. No.	Response	Number	Percentage
1.	Skill acquisition	39	92.85
2.	Earning money	21	50.00

Note: Four parents were not included as they were against it.

Awareness about child Labour Laws

Every society has its own pattern of life suited to their livelihood. This pattern of life in the old society was regulated through its norms. Social norms and values are upheld by an approved machinery of the society to regulate and maintain the social order. In a complex society, where social system is easily broken, it becomes much more difficult to maintain the social system. In such situations, formal law is helpful. The major functions of the legal system are (Gangrad-1982)

1. Maintenance of public order
2. Upholding rights and duties
3. Facilitating co-operation
4. Confirming legitimacy
5. Communicating normal standards.

Law is always helpful in protecting the poor and the needy. In every society, old traditions, values and norms create difficulty in adopting new changes for development and growth of its members. Therefore, reformation is needed to change its old system to meet the needs for their welfare and development. Long ago, child labour was not a social problem, but with the change in social understanding, child labour needed legislative protection against their exploitation and for their proper growth and development.

To protect children from the adverse affects of employment especially on their physical and mental development, there are several laws in India. These laws are either derived from the Indian Constitution or from the International Labour Organization (ILO) recommendations, or from the declaration of the Rights of the Child unanimously adopted by the General Assembly of the United Nations on Nov. 20th, 1959.

Infact there is a mass support for the abolition of child labour on the part of the state as well as the society. But the people who are directly involved in the occupation i.e. child labourers; their parents and their employers have different opinions. Our investigations revealed that majority of the child labourers were unaware of the child labour laws.

Abolition of Child Labour

Most of the people vehemently oppose employment of children in any sort of job. Child labour is a shameful scan on the nation. According to them, these children are denied their childhood care, comforts, play, training and education. Child labour is a contradictory term, since children are not supposed to work. So it should be abolished altogether. Others are of the opinion that in the present Indian context total abolition of child labour is not possible. According to them abolition of child labour will throw millions of destitute children to destruction. They have proposed some measures by which their working conditions may be improved. About 43 (61.42%) of sampled parents/guardian are in favour of the abolition of child labour whereas 27 (38.57%) were against the abolition of child labour.

Views about the Abolition of Child Labour

The sampled parents/guardians of the child labourers provide different view points for the eradication of the problem from the society. The views of parents/guardians are recorded in below mentioned table (6.35).

Table 6.35: Views of Parents about the Abolition of Child Labour

S. No.	Views	Number	Percentage
1.	Help financially to poor people	53	75.71
2.	Govt. job to one of the members of the family of child labourers	38	54.28
3.	Punishment to persons who employ children	44	62.85
4.	Scholarships to poor students	47	67.14
5.	Fine both to parents and employers of child labourers	35	50.00
6.	Child labourers should be forcibly sent to school	23	32.85

Source: Field Study 2009.

It is generally known that there is a mass support for the abolition of child labour on the part of the state as well as the society. About 53 (75.71%) parents expressed their view point as to help poor people financially and the institution of child labour will abolish itself. Government job to one of the members of the families of child labourers, punishment to persons who employ children, scholarship should be given to poor students and the problem will come to its minimum level or will get abolish totally responded the sampled parents. Another group of parents 35 (50.00%) responded that there should be fine both on the parents and employers of the child labourers whereas equally percentage of parents responded that child labourers should be forcibly sent to school.

Sending Children to School

In the preceding situation, there were significant numbers of child labourers who may like to attend the school or work in the unit/centre and attend the school simultaneously. Thus, in our investigation, the response of the parents reflects that 53 (75.71%) will send their children to school if such opportunity comes or will be given. The parents/guardians who were against of sending their children to school inspite of the opportunity given/will come disclosed the reasons noted in the following table 6.36.

Table 6.36: Classification of Parental Reasons not Sending their Children to School if the Opportunity Comes

S. No.	*Reasons*	*Number*	*Percentage*
1.	Earlier skill acquisition	17	100.00
2.	Finding hard to educate children	13	76.47
3.	To provide education to girls is fruitless	11	64.70

Source: Field Study 2009.

Role of Community in the Elimination of Child Labour

It was found that though art and craft pieces produced by the child labourers were highly appreciated, their work in the units/centres as well as in the homes was condemned. It was in the context of this situation in which the child labourers left the school and joined the working units/centres. Thus, the child labour was portrayed as undesirable for these children belonged to the tender age group and instead of working in the units/centres or homes the general feeling is that, they should have been in the schools. In this situational context, majority of the sampled parents favoured that community can play its role in the elimination of child labour through following (table 6.37) measures.

Table 6.37: Reasons for How Community can Play its Role in the Elimination of Child Labour by Parents

S. No.	*Reason*	*Number*	*Percentage*
1.	Through restriction	34	48.57
2.	Through awareness	43	61.42
3.	Through NGO's	19	27.14
4.	Through GO's	47	67.14
5.	Through financial help to poor families	58	82.85

Source: Field Study 2009.

Role of Employers in the Elimination of Child Labour

Children provide cheap and convenient labour. They are non-complaining labour force who can made to do any work for any amount of time, wages less than what is paid to their adult counterparts on the plea that they are less efficient. Their requirements are few and they learn on the job. But by observation the sampled employers showed a different kind of interest as according to them they would like the end of child labour in Kashmir. It was in this situational context that we asked them if they can play any role in the elimination of the child labour. The table (6.38) shows the response.

Table 6.38: Role of Employers in the Elimination of Child Labour

S. No.	*Employers Role*	*Number*	*Percentage*
1.	No employment to children	14	40.00
2.	Create awareness	29	82.85
3.	Inform authorities	13	37.14
4.	Motivate them to go to school	23	65.71

Source: Field Study 2008-09.

Role of Governmental and Non-governmental Organizations

Government of India has enacted a number of legislations which prohibit and regulate the employment and working conditions of the child labourers in various occupations and vocations. The fact stands that the government and its organizations ought to work for the safety, security and betterment of people. However this role has become controversial in the context of practices of corruption. The children also have developed particular attitudes towards the government, in general, and towards its organizations, in particular. In this background, when approached a dominant majority of the employers have very good information about GOs and NGOs help. The following table (6.39) highlights the role of GOs in the elimination of child labour.

Table 6.39: Employers' Opinion about the Role of GOs in the Elimination of Child Labour

S. No.	Response	Number	Percentage
1.	Legislation implementation	12	34.28
2.	Compulsory schooling	23	65.71
3.	Provide training	13	37.14
4.	All the above	11	31.42

Source: Field Study 2009.

NGO's Initiative

On the other hand, the NGO's also work in the field to stop and completely eradicate the institution of child labour. They want child labourers to go to schools and try hard to motivate the out-of-school children to return to school. But, their role has not been understood properly and there is hardly any awareness found among the Child labourers, parents and even employers about the NGO's. Their response shows that they have never heard the name of the NGO's. In their response they are quite clear and categorical about the role of the NGO's. Almost all the employers 33 (94.28%) responded that the NGO's should help financially to families of child labourers which to our understanding no NGO can do.

Focused Cases

Apart from serving the written schedules, we also followed the method of observation and maintained the field diary during the field work. During the course of field work, we observed some striking facts about the child labour. We witnessed some special cases of child labourers which highlighted the nature, causes and consequences of the problem. The study of these cases will certainly lead to a deeper and wider sociological understanding of the phenomenon of child labour.

Special Case–1

An eye opener case during the field visit came to our notice was that of a girl who was only thirteen years old. She was engaged in handicrafts work at a very young age. She narrated the facts as to how she was forced to join this work. Actually her mother was engaged in this work but God loved her more than any body and took her into his custody. There was nobody in the family to take the work/tradition. Therefore, finding no option, she stepped into the shoes of her mother and started handicrafts work to maintain the tradition of the family as she was elder in family. She further narrated that she earns very little which is usually spent on family requirements. She has always this apprehension that like her mother she may not went into the custody of God at a very young age.

Special Case–2

Ruqaya nick named Payal is a teenager. She belongs to Qazigund block of south Kashmir district Islamabad. She is always on work from early morning to late evening. While narrating her story, she said that she was only seven and a half years old when she joined the handicrafts work. Her parents forcibly put her into this work. As in their locality/area it is a tradition to send female child/children at a very tender age for work. She has to perform both domestic as well as handicrafts work.

She wakes up before dawn, to prepare tea and breakfast for

everyone in the family including her parents and siblings. She is the elder daughter of their parents. Then she washes the previous night's utensils and brings water from a good distance for the day's use. Again she has to bring water in the evening for drinking and other purposes. As she completes the work in the morning at home, she then leaves for handicraft centre where she performs the handicrafts work upto evening. She also brings it to our notice that many a times she would take the unfinished work to home and complete it upto midnight. She hands over all the earnings to her father and does not keep anything with her.

Ruqaya was very much interested in studies but her parents were having other ideas for her. One could easily observe desperation current on her innocent young face. When she was asked if the opportunity will be given for studying will she go. Her answer was no, as she has lost interest in studies and will feel ashamed with little children in the class at this age.

Special Case–3

Gulshan, a girl of thirteen years resides in a far flung village of Budgam. She belongs to a very poor family. For maintaining the delicate balance of the family budget and to keep the wolf away from the door, her parents had no alternative but to send her into the handicrafts work to save the family from a shipwreck. Her house has two bedrooms and a kitchen with common hall. It takes her around one and half an hour to do dusting, sweeping and mopping. She has also to do the most arduous work, i.e. hand washing of clothes early in the morning before leaving for handicrafts work. She works almost eight hours a day and six days in a week with water, the only facility available in the handicraft centre. During off-days she carries domestic and agricultural work in the family.

Paid very less for her labour; working in unhygienic conditions with no health security narrated the innocent poor girl with a desperate voice. She would like to attend school rather than handicrafts work but the condition at home and the need to supplement the family income stops her from doing so. She is also aware that working at this age will affect not her present only but the future too and is working now with the intention to make the future of her siblings secure by not allowing anything to become an impediment in their schooling. She loves to leave the work if the alternative is provided and dreams to be a rich person in future so that she can break the bond between child labour and her family.

7

CONCLUSIONS AND SUGGESTIONS

The main objective of the present study has been to study child labour in the traditional and transitional Kashmiri society. The study has been undertaken among child labourers in the different sectors of the economy in order to establish the phenomenon of child labour in its proper perspective. The objectives of the study have been fulfilled by projecting appropriate variables in the process of data analysis and discussion. Each and every variable taken into account has been in a position to examine the plight of child labourers in the various sectors. The major findings and conclusions that emerged from the analysis and discussion on the question of child labour in Kashmir are centred on the pathology of an institution, around which many laws have been passed and the commissions which have drawn attention to this malpractice from time to time. The study also successfully discusses the findings where the issues involved in child labour based on a well designed methodology are debated. However, the truth is, the thesis communicates that the poverty of people forces them to continue to send young children to work.

A wider range of aspects such as family, economic status, parental perception, education, gender discrimination, middle men dimension and exploitation, relations of production, cultural acceptance, and issues of health and recreation, etc. are discussed adeptly in the main body of the manuscript. The study specially concentrates on existing rules, and the breaking of these rules. Within that framework, the study has valuable data on family structure, poverty and its indexes including level of education, occupation and health, as parameters of understanding the life of these children. The health conditions are particularly bad as the careful reading shows by understanding the life chances of these children who work on carpets, papier mache, agriculture, streets, hotels and restaurants and other objects which are an integral part of the tourist trade. Infact, the study has done a careful statistical analysis of many different aspects of child labourers in Kashmir with a special focus on qualitative indexes which gives a sense of the relations between town and country, between tourism and political environments, between commerce and consumption and human rights. Apart from these, certain important suggestions are made to ameliorate the problem of child labour in contemporary society.

Conclusions

They are tiny apostles of peace but we forget that they are, at first, very much human beings though young. In the long run strength, prosperity, future and dignity of a society depend to a great extent upon how its children are brought up and trained.

According to Maria Montessori "Humanity shows itself in all its intellectual splendour during this tender age as the sun shows itself at the dawn, and the flower in the first enfolding of the petals, and we must respect religiously, reverently, these first indications of individuality. If any educational act is to be efficacious, it will be only that which tends to help towards the complete unfolding of this life."

After the birth of the child, problem which nation faces are nutritious food to both mother and child, vaccination and general medical care, legitimacy, nationality, physical and social environment, education, recreation, prevention of exploitation and hazards, bonded labour, child abduction, child labour, misuse of abducted children for smuggling and other nefarious activities, like physical and mental torture.

The problem of child labour has assumed menacing magnitude and intensity during the twentieth century and continues even in the present era. The present study clearly revealed that the problem of child labour in Kashmiri society has wider ramifications. Taking into consideration the causes and consequences of the problem, the situation reflects an extremely cruel social situation which engulfs socially, economically and educationally backward communities. The problem of child labour as existing in Kashmiri society has given rise to multidimensional problems having adverse implications on one's physical, social, emotional, mental, moral and educational development. It is not only social apathy towards child labour but the government in this regard has also shown lack of interest; thereby the problem has become more complex and dangerous. Moreover, problem of social control, crime and social conflict emanate from the situation with out proper care and response, on the part of government and the society at large.

Any social problem as an empirical reality has various aspects, such as demographic, economic, geographic, psychological and social. This study has tried to highlight the social aspect of the problem of the working children using techniques of data collection accepted by sociologists and presenting it in terms and concepts used in sociological writings.

On the basis of the findings of the study, one can safely conclude that:

1. The practice of child labour is primarily found among the socio-economically weaker sections of society with wide spread illiteracy and ignorance, of the people of the society. Lack of quality education contributes significantly for the emergence and growth of child labour in the present modern educational values.
2. The working conditions of the child labourers in the various sectors are grossly detrimental to the growth and development of the child labourers who are totally deprived of the minimum requirements.
3. The socio-economically poor children are subjected to exploitation in the handicrafts work.
4. Abolition of child labour totally is not favoured by parents and employers for economic and other reasons.
5. No working unit/centre has socio-political awareness.

The research findings reveal clearly that the problem of child labour is rooted deep in Kashmiri society. Tremendous growth in population accompanied by poverty, illiteracy and ignorance and lack of quality education, etc. are the major causes responsible for child labour. It adversely affects one's personality in terms of its physical, social, emotional, moral and educational development. The study shows that no one is showing concern towards the problem of child labour. Their insecure childhood makes them more vulnerable to exploitation. They face inhuman attitude on the part of their employers. They work in very much dirty environment. Though there are various laws to abolish child labour but they always remain confined to papers as reflected by the action of the government.

Last, but not the least, the question arises, whether child labour can be abolished. If yes, how.

The present study indicates that total abolition of child labour is neither possible nor desirable so long as there is wide spread poverty, illiteracy and ignorance and unemployment, etc. Far from solving problem, its total abolition will further aggravate it. Following are some of the suggestions suggested for the solution of the problem.

Suggestions for Solution

1. The first approach is defining implementation of the provisions of different legislations. More inspecting officials with intensive inspection are needed for the purpose. The officials should work sincerely being aware of the seriousness of the problem.
2. There is dire need to impart education to the child workers. Though child workers cannot attend normal school during the usual school hours, the only alternative is to provide them some agency of education at the time when they are free. The constitutional obligation to provide free and compulsory education to all children up to fourteen years must be fulfilled without any further delay. There should be special schemes for development of socially and educationally disadvantaged groups of the society.
3. Governmental and non-governmental organizations should organize awareness programmes regarding the consequences of child labour and motivate common people, village heads, teachers and other employers, senior citizens, etc. and seek their cooperation in respective areas to serve the purpose.
4. It has also been observed in the field that the female child labourers are not paid equal to the male child labourers. This and other differentiation must be finished immediately.

5. Poor families whose children are involved in handicrafts work, etc. should be supported with credit linked rural development programmes for taking up suitable micro business, especially by male members in view of economic betterment, which would lead a direct attack on poverty.
6. Provision for weekly leave with wage should be regulated and implemented by the employers. Non-compliance of such rules should amount to punishment of unit/centre owners, middlemen and labour officials. For this purpose, an appropriate monitoring authority can be created by involving government officials, NGOs and local bodies.
7. Children should be provided non-formal job oriented education so that it enhances their skills, which would enable them to shift to more remunerative satisfaction and less hazardous alternative employment.
8. Media should play its role in generating awareness among the people regarding the upliftment and betterment of socially, economically and educationally backward communities by providing them information regarding various programmes and schemes launched by the government for their upliftment.
9. The basic and necessary facilities/conditions must be provided to the child labourers working in the handicraft centres. This is must for the quality work on the part of child labourers; while the former refers to the facilities like heating, water, electricity, and entertainment and so on, the later includes high standard of salaries and regular payment of the wages to the child labourers.
10. The most important approach relates to socio-economic factors, which are the basic reasons of the problems. It would be mainly preventive of the problem and promotive of growth opportunities for children. These can be taken care of by: (1) Effective implementation of integrated child development schemes, shall be helpful in lessening the burden of poor parents for child grooming and in building a healthy foundation for all pre-school children in terms of better health care, nutrition and education. (2) Attractive and free pre and primary school education system is necessary to attract children towards education instead of work and income. Community based school extension programme, i.e. to make people aware of benefits

and necessity of education, to encourage and convince children to go to schools is essential, etc.

11. The most basic public intervention to eliminate child labour is the provision of free, compulsory and good quality education. A greater degree of public outrage and social action is required to make any counter strategy really effective.
12. The scope of Child Labour (Prohibition and Regulation) Act, 1986, should be extended with a view to cover establishments of all types were any kind of work is carried on by the owners with the help of children. Efforts must be made to extend the scope of the Act to cover unorganized sector, such as handicraft units, etc.
13. Non-governmental organizations (NGOs) and other related agencies have to play vital role to make aware the down–trodden communities regarding the rights of children and harmful effects of child labour.
14. Government should take up steps and consult scholars, academicians, planners belonging to different streams in order to frame policies about the future and overall development of these unfortunate children.

BIBLIOGRAPHY

Arya, Sadhna. 2000. *Women, Gender Equality and the State*. New Delhi. Deep and Deep Publishers.

Anandharajakumar, P. 2004. *Female Child Labour*. New Delhi. APH Publishing Corporation.

Arora, R.C. 1989. *In the land of Kashmir, Ladakh and Gilgit*. Srinagar. Gulshan Publishers.

Ashok, K. Srivastava. 1998. *Child Development: The Indian Perspective*. New Delhi. Publication Division, National Council at Global Computers.

Bahura, N.K. and R.P. Mohanty. 2005. *Status and Empowerment of the Girl Child–Aspects in Cross–Cultural Context*. New Delhi. Discovery Publishing House.

Bhargava, Pramila H. 2003. *The Elimination of Child Labour: Whose Responsibility*. New Delhi. Sage Publications.

Boal, A. 1985. *The Theatre of the Oppressed*. London. Pluto Press.

Burra, N. 1995. "*Born to Work: Child Labour in India*". Oxford University Press.

Chohan, Amar Singh. 1983. *Historical Study of Society and Culture in Dardistan and Ladakh*. New Delhi. Atlantic Publishers.

Cuningham, Alexander. 1997. *Ladakh–Physical, Statistical and Historical*. Gulshan Publishers. Srinagar.

Cunningham, H. 1991. *The Children of The Poor*. Oxford. Blackwell.

D' Souza, Alfred. 1995. *Children in India–Critical Issues in Human Development*. New Delhi. Social Institute.

Desai, A.R. 1984. *Capitalist Path of Development*. Bombay. Popular Prakasan.

Devasia, Leelama and V.V. Devasia. 1991. *Girl Child in India*. New Delhi. Ashish Publishing House.

Devi, Laxmi. 1998. *Encyclopaedia of Child and Family Welfare*. vol. 4. New Delhi. Institute of Sustainable Development Lucknow and Anmol Publications Pvt. Ltd.

Dewan, Pervez. 2004. *Jammu. Kashmir and Ladakh-Kashmir*. New Delhi. Manas Publications.

Dewan, Pervez. 2004. *Jammu. Kashmir and Ladakh-Ladakh*. New Delhi. Manas Publications.

Dingwancy, M. *et al*. 1988. *Children of Darkness: A Manual on Child Labour in India*. New Delhi. Rural Labour Cell. NLI.

Elias, Mendelievich. 1979. *Children at Work*. Geneva. ILO.

Francke, A.H. 1977. *A History of Ladakh*. New Delhi. Sterling Publishers Pvt. Ltd.

Ghosh, A. 1985. *Humanizing Child Labour*. Calcutta. IPER.

Gokhale, D. Sharad and Sohoni K. Neera. 1979. *Child in India*. Bombay. Somaiya Publications Pvt. Ltd.

Goyal. P.K. 2005. *Street Children and the Child Labour*. Delhi. Vista International Publishing House.

Gupta, M. and K. Voll. 1987. *Young Hands at Work*. New Delhi. Atma Ram and Sons.

Gurusamy, S. 1995. *Child Labour–Causes and Factors*. New Delhi. Sterling Publishers Pvt. Ltd.

Hassnain, F.M. Masato Oki. and Tokan D. Sumi. 1997. *Ladakh–The Moon Land*. New Delhi. Light and Life Publishers.

Haxton, P. 1984. *An Analysis of the Situation of Children in India*. New Delhi. UNICEF.

Holland, P. 1992. *What Is A Child*. London. Virago Press.

Hussnain, F.M. 1980. *Heritage of Kashmir*. Srinagar. Kashmir. Gulshan Publishers.

Ivy, George. 1990. *Child Labour and Child Work*. New Delhi. Ashish Publishing House.

Jenks, Chris. 1982. *The Sociology of Childhood–Essential Readings*. London. Batsford Academic and Educational Ltd.

Jha, K.J. 2002. *Status of Girl Child in India*. New Delhi. Sarup and Sons.

Jina, Prem Singh. 1996. *Ladakh–The Land and The People*. New Delhi. Indus Publishing Company.

Jina, Prem Singh. 2000. *Ladakh–Past and Present*. New Delhi. Gyan Publishing House.

Juyal, B.N. *et al*. 1985. *Child Labour: The Twice Exploited*. Varanasi. Gandhian Institute of Studies.

Kanbagri, Ramesh. 1991. *Child Labour in the Indian Sub-continent: Dimensions and Implications*. New Delhi. Sage Publications.

Kapur, M.L. 1992. *Social and Economic History of Jammu and Kashmir State*. New Delhi. Anmol Publications.

Kaul, M.N. and P.N. Chopra. 1992. *Encyclopedia of India. Volume X (J&K): Ladakh*. New Delhi. Rima Publishing House.

Kaul, Shridhar and H.N. Kaul. 1992. *Ladakh Through The Ages–Towads a New Identity*. New Delhi. Indus Publishing Company.

Khatu, K. *et al*. 1993. *Working Children in India*. Baroda. ORG.

Kulshreshtha, C. Jinesh. 1994. *Indian Child Labour*. New Delhi. Uppal Publishing House.

Kumar, Arun. 2002. *Child as Human Resource–Policies and Approaches*. New Delhi. Sarup and Sons.

Kumar, Ashok. *Developing Women and Children in India*. New Delhi. Common Wealth Publishers.

Kumar, R. 1988. *Child Development in India: Health. Welfare and Management*. New Delhi. Ashish Publishing House.

Kusuma, A. 1997. *Child Rearing Practices in Tribals*. New Delhi. Discovery Publishing House.

Lidhoo, Lal Moti. 1987. *Kashmir Tribals: Child Rearing and Psycho-social Development*. New Delhi. Ashish Publishing House.

McCandless, R. Boyd and Ellis D. Ecans. 1973. *Child and Youth–Psychological Development*. Hinsdale Illionis. The Dryden Press.

Mehta, P.L. and S.S. Jaswal. 1996. *Child Labour and The Law-Myth and Reality of Child Welfare*. New Delhi. Deep and Deep Publications.

Metha, P.L. and S.S. Jaswal. 1997. *Child Labour and Law*. New Delhi. Deep and Deep Publications.

Ministry of Social Welfare, Government of India. New Delhi. 1980. *Profile of The Child in India: Policies and Programmes*. New Delhi. Rekha Printers Private Ltd.

Mishra, G.P. and P.N. Pande. 1996. *Child Labour in Carpet Industry*. New Delhi. APH Publishing Corporation.

Mishra, Lakshmidhar. 2000. *Child Labour in India*. New Delhi. Oxford University Press.

Mishra, S.N. and Sweta Mishra. 2004. *Tiny Hands in the Unorganized Sector*. Delhi. Shipra Publications.

Mittal, Sujata. 2004. *Child Development*. Delhi. Usha Books.

Mowli, Chandra V. 1992. *Jogin–Girl Child Labour Studies*. New Delhi. Sterling Publishers Pvt. Ltd.

Mustafa, Mohd. and Onkar Sharma. 2003. *Child Labour in India: A Bitter Truth*. New Delhi. Deep and Deep Publications Pvt. Ltd.

Naido, U.S. and K.R. Kapadia. (eds.). 1985. *Child Labour and Health: Problems and Prospects*. Bombay. Tata Institute of Social Sciences.

Narasaiah, Lakshmi M. 2006. *Child Labour and Education*. New Delhi. Discovery Publishing House.

Nieuwenhuys, O. 1994. *Children's Lifeworlds: Gender. Welfare and Labour in the Developing World.* London. Routledge.

Pandit, M. Amin. 1997. *Ladakh–Land of Possessive Powers and Charm.* Srinagar. Gulshan Publishers.

Pati, R.N. 1989. *Rehabilitation of Child Labourers in India.* New Delhi. Ashish Publishing House.

Patil, B.R. 1988. *Working Children in Urban India.* Bangalore. D.B. Publishers Pvt. Ltd.

Punecha, L.B. 2006. *Child Labour: A Social Evil.* New Delhi. Alfa Publications.

Rane, Asha. 1994. *Street Children: A Challenge to The Social Work Profession.* Tata Institute of Social Sciences. Bombay. Published by Sheilu Srinivasan.

Rao, Malini. 2000. *Socialization of Children and Youth.* Agra. National Psychological Corporation.

Rao, prasada M. 2006. *Child Labour: Problems and Policy Issues.* Ambala. The Associated Publishers.

Reddy, Y.S. 2000. *Child Labour.* New Delhi. Anmol Publications Pvt. Ltd.

Sagwal, S.S. *Ladakh–Ecology and Environment.* New Delhi. Ashish Publishing House.

Saksena, Anu. 2000. *Human Rights and Child Labour in Indian Industries.* Delhi. Shipra Publication.

Sanon, S. Chandragupt. 1998. *Working Children: A Sociological Analysis.* New Delhi. APH Publishing Corporation.

Sapra, Rekha. 2006. *Child Development: Issues and Concerns For The Well Being of The Child.* New Delhi. Vishvabharti Publications.

Satyarthi, Kailash and Bupinder Zutshi. 2006. *Globalisation. Development and Child Rights.* Delhi. Shipra Publications.

Shah, Nazir Ahmed. 1992. *Child Labour in India.* New Delhi. Anmol Publications.

Sharma, B.K. and V. Mittar. 1990. *Child Labour and Urban Formal Sector.* New Delhi. Deep and Deep Publications.

Sharma, Usha. 2006. *Female Labour in India.* New Delhi. Mittal Publications.

Shukla, C.K. and S. Ali. 2006. *Child Labour: Socio-Economic Dimensions.* New Delhi. Sarup and Sons.

Singh, A.N. 1990. *Child Labour in India: Socio-Economic Perspectives.* Delhi. Shipra Publications.

Singh, A.N. 1996. *The Child Rag–Pickers: Socio-Economic Perspectives and Intervention Strategies.* Delhi. Shipra Publications.

Singh, I.S. 1992. *Child Labour.* New Delhi. Oxford and IBH Publishing Co. Pvt. Ltd.

Shirur Prachi. 2007. Education Child Labour and NGOs. Delhi. Shipra Publications.

Singh, M. *et al.* 1980. *Working Children in Bombay: A Study.* New Delhi. NIPCCD.

Singh, Musafir. 1975. *Working Children in Bombay–Combating Child Labour*. Geneva. Indian Labour Press.

Srinivasan, K. *et al*. 1979. *Demographic and Socio–Economic Aspects of Child in India*. Bombay. Himalaya Publishing House.

Sumi, T.D. 1997. *Ladakh–The Moon Land*. New Delhi. Light and Life Publishers.

Tripathy, S.K. 1989. *Child Labour in India*. New Delhi. Discovery Publishing House.

Tripathy, S.N. 1996. *Child Labour in India: Issues and Policy Options*. New Delhi. Discovery Publishing House.

Varandani, Gursharan. 1994. *Child Labour and Women Workers*. New Delhi. Ashish Publishing House.

Vasta, R. 1979. *Studying Children: An Introduction to Research Methods*. San Francisco. W.H. Freeman.

Weiner, M. 1991. *The Child and The State in India*. Princeton. Princeton Press.

WHO. 1987. *Children at Work: Special Health Risks*. Geneva. ILO.

Zutshi, Bhupinder. 2002. *In the Name of Child Labour*. Delhi. Shipra Publication.

Articles

Ali, Nisar. 1987. *Child Labour in the Carpet Industry of Kashmir*. In: M. Gupta (eds.). Child Labour in India. Delhi. Atma Ram and Sons Publication.

Kumar, P. 1964. *Child Labour: A Socio-Legal Study*. Journal of the Indian Law Institute. pp. 27-33.

Lynn, S. Liben. Volume 77. Number 4. July/August 2006. *Child Development*. USA. Blackwell Publishing–Malden. pp. 5-7.

National Association for Gifted Children. 2006. Volume 50. Number 3. *Gifted Child*. Published NAGC Washington D.C. p. 9.

Reddy, N. 1988. *Blossoms in the Dust*. 3 (7). The Lawyers Collectives.

Springer. May 2000. *Maternal and Child Health Journal*. Volume 10. Number 3-New York. USA. pp. 3-5.

Reports

"Our Voices... Are You Listening". 2006. Children's Committees for Village Development (Ladakh*)*. Save the Children. UK.

Banerjee, S. 1979. *Child Labour in India. A General Review—With Case Studies of the Brick Making and Zari Embroidery Industries*. No. 2.

Child Labour Research in Kashmir Valley. 2001. *Adphail Golab—Unbloomed Roses*. Save the Children. U.K.

Dabla, B.A. 2006-07. *Life Conditions of Child Labourers in the Handicraft Sector in Kashmir*. report prepared for ICSSR. New Delhi.

Gupta, M. 1989. *Child Labour in Hazardous Work in India: Situation and Policy Experience*. study conducted for the ILO. Geneva.

Kanbargi, Ramesh. 1985. *Children Working in the Carpet Factories of the Varanasi District in Uttar Pradesh*. In: Baqute and J. Boyden (eds.).

Kutay, Nazir Ahmad and Miss Sabhia Malik. 2002. *Causes and Consequences of Child Labour in Kashmir*. report prepared for. Reflections: A Compilation of Research Studies' J&K State Resource Centre. University of Kashmir–Srinagar.

Naidu, S. and Kamen. 1985. *Child Labour: Problems and Prospectus*. Tata Institute of Social Sciences. Bombay.

Nangia, S. 1993. *Child workers in the Carpet Weaving Industry in J&K*. Noida. Child Labour Publication Cell.

Sapru, H.L. *Carpet Weaving–A World Perspective Craft*. Jammu and Kashmir. Directorate of Handicrafts.

Other Papers

Boyden, J. 1994. *The Relationship Between Education and Child Work*. Child Rights Series. No. 4.

Menon, Amarnath K. and Stephen David. Dec. 18, 2006. *Children on Sale: The Agony of Kalhandi*. India Today.

Morrow, V. 2003. *A Look at the Hand–Made Carpet Industry With Particular Reference to India and Kashmir*. Streetwise International Cambridge.

Internet Sources

www.antislavery.org

www.bbc.co.uk

www.globalmarch.org

www.ilo.org

www.ipec.org

www.savethechildren.org.uk

www.shareholderaction.org

www.ucw-project.org

www.un.org

www.unesco.org

www.unicef.org

www.workingchild.org

www.worldbank.org

INDEX